laurie polich-short
STUDIES ON THE GO

GENESIS

  youth specialties

ZONDERVAN.com/
AUTHOR**TRACKER**
follow your favorite authors

We want to hear from you. Please send your comments about this
book to us in care of zreview@zondervan.com. Thank you.

ZONDERVAN

Studies on the Go: Genesis
Copyright © 2012 by Laurie Polich-Short

YS Youth Specialties is a trademark of YOUTHWORKS!, INCORPORATED and is registered
with the United States Patent and Trademark Office.

This title is also available as a Zondervan ebook. Visit www.zondervan.com/ebooks.

Requests for information should be addressed to:

Zondervan, *Grand Rapids, Michigan 49530*

ISBN 978-0-310-88983-0

Cover design: Toolbox Studios
Interior design: SharpSeven Design/David Conn

Printed in the United States of America

12 13 14 15 16 /DCI/ 22 21 20 19 18 17 16 15 14 13 12 11 10 9 8 7 6 5 4 3 2 1

DEDICATION

To Jere and Jordan Short—God's great story for my life.

ACKNOWLEDGMENTS

The OH staff: Jon Ireland, Jono Shaffer, Uriah Venegas, Cosy Del Carlo, Ryan Warner, Johnny Miller, and Ashley Maddox: I appreciate doing life and ministry with you.

Vivian McIlraith, June Michealsen, and Renee Curtis: Mentors who've encouraged me to listen to God and live my story.

Melissa Johnston, Stacy Sharpe, Vicki Stairs, and Marlo Blanford: Friends who walk with me on the journey.

Ramona, Synicka, Timothy, Jane, Joseph, Nica, and Jordan: Some of the great God stories of my life.

CONTENTS

INTRODUCTION

Genesis is a book of stories—and these stories have power to change our lives. While the stories are about certain people from a certain time, they carry messages for *all* people at *all* times. That is why this book is so important.

The stories in Genesis unfold the beginnings of human life. They also show us God's role in creating and orchestrating life.

And in these Studies on the Go, your students will be introduced to people whose lives became part of a much, much bigger story—all because they let God lead them.

Your students will be challenged to do the same.

But it's through the questions in this book (not the answers) that your students will explore the book of Genesis. The hope is that through wrestling with these questions, students (and you, too) will discover more about who God is—and how our lives can be used for purposes that outlive us.

There are 30 studies in this book, designed to be digested one week at a time (although you can go through the book however it best suits you and your group).

These 30 sessions will take you through the entire book of Genesis. More time is dedicated to some passages as opposed to others, but your students will gain a solid grasp of the whole book of Genesis when you're through.

As with the other books in the Studies on the Go series:

- Each session begins with Share questions (to introduce your students to the theme of the text and break the ice a little);

- Then Observation questions (to get your students familiar with the text);

- Interpretation questions (to help your students think about the text);

- and Application questions (to encourage your students to live the text).

Finally, there's an optional exercise at the end of each session to help your students apply the message of the session. And there are also reproducible Quiet Time Reflections at the end of each session that you can give to students so they can dig deeper into the Bible on their own, applying that week's session every day of that week.

Again, remember to take on the parts of this book that suit your group best. You don't have to use every question in the book, and you can feel free to add to them or alter them depending on what your group needs.

From Genesis we learn that hope comes from struggle, perseverance comes from pain, and life is found in letting go. My prayer is that these stories will inspire your students to live their stories well—not only for themselves, but also for the parts they will play in God's story.

That's the reason we're here, after all.

1. IN THE BEGINNING
Genesis 1

"In the beginning, God *created*."

Genesis 1 reveals how. With the words "And God said" the power of God's word is demonstrated. God spoke—and it came to be. Light and darkness. Earth and sky. Plants and trees. Stars and sunshine. Fish and birds. You and me.

God said, "Let there be . . ." and there was.

The first 26 verses of Genesis 1 describe how God created life. But the last seven verses show that God gave responsibility for that life to us. God declared us rulers of creation, and because of that we have the power to plant trees and give birth to babies and cure diseases.

But we also have the power to kill and destroy and bring death.

One look at the way we've handled this power makes us question whether human beings were worthy of such responsibility.

God believed that we were.

Perhaps that is the greatest miracle of all.

IN THE BEGINNING: GENESIS 1

Share

Warm-Up Qs (Use one or more as needed depending on your group)

- If someone asked you to describe how you suppose the world began, how would you answer?

- While you were growing up, were you taught to agree with divine creation or the theory of evolution? Which view best represents what you agree with now?

- What evidence of God's creative power do you see in the world around you? Is there any place in the world around you where you feel closest to God? Why?

Observe

Observation Qs

- According to vv. 1-2, what information do we have about how the earth came to be? What information do we have about God from these verses? What information don't we have?

- As you observe vv. 3, 6, 9, 14, 20, and 24, what do they all have in common? How did God create the world?

- What was the order of creation? (What did God create first? What did God create last?) Is there any verse in Genesis 1 that is confusing to you?

- What do you observe in vv. 26-30 about the creation of human beings? What tasks did God give us to do?

Think

Interpretation Qs

- According to Genesis 1, there were six "days" of Creation. But v. 14 says God introduced the measurement of seasons, days, and years. Do you believe the six days of creation were the same length as our days? Why/why not?

- How does God view the objects of his creation? How do we know? Did God say anything different after he created us?

What clues do we have in this chapter about God's feelings in regard to creating the world and us?

- Look at Genesis 1:26-27. Do you wonder if God created only men in his image—or men and women? Why? What do you suppose it means to be created in God's image?

- Why do you suppose God says, "Let us make mankind in our image?" (v. 26) Why does God use plural language?

Apply

Application Qs

- If someone asked if you believe the earth and human race were divinely created, how would you respond?

- What part(s) of the biblical creation account are difficult for you to understand? What parts are easy for you to understand?

- As you consider the tasks God has given humans to do on this earth (vv. 26-30), how do you rate our performance? Do you suppose God is pleased or disappointed with how we've managed the world around us? What grade do you give yourself as a manager of creation?

- When you think about being made in God's image, how does that affect the way you feel about yourself? Do you feel more like a mistake or a masterpiece? Why?

Do

Optional Activity

Gather magazines and newspapers and put them in the middle of your group. Distribute pieces of poster board or construction paper and have your group cut out and paste (on one side of the paper) words and images that represent how they see themselves; on the other side should be words and images that represent how God created them to be. Have your students share if there are differences between the way they see themselves and the way God sees them—and why.

QUIET TIME REFLECTIONS

Day 1: Genesis 1:1-5

- What word or verse stands out to you from this passage? Why?

- How did God start creating the heavens and the earth? What did God use to create?

- Spend time today thinking about the power of God's word— and what kind of power it has in your life.

Day 2: Genesis 1:6-13

- What word or verse stands out to you from this passage? Why?

- What did the earth first look like when God created the sky? When did trees first appear?

- Spend time today thinking about what the earth looked like after the third day.

Day 3: Genesis 1:13-19

- What word or verse stands out to you from this passage? Why?

- Where did seasons come from? What is the "light to govern the day" that God created for us?

- Spend time today thinking about what the earth would be like without the sun—and thank God for its light and warmth.

Day 4: Genesis 1:20-25

- What word or verse stands out to you from this passage? Why?

- Where did God first create living creatures? What were they?

- Spend time today thinking about the different fish and animals God has created—and how they reflect God's artistry.

Day 5: Genesis 1:26-28

- What word or verse stands out to you from these verses? Why?

- What two commands does God give man and woman? What does this tell you about God's love for us?

- Spend time today thinking about God's love expressed to us through creation.

Day 6: Genesis 1:29-31

- What word or verse stands out to you from these verses? Why?

- How does God feel about creation when he's through? Do you suppose God still feels that way?

- Spend time today thinking about how you have appreciated God for creation. What can you be thankful for today?

Day 7: Genesis 1

Read through the whole chapter and write out the verse or passage that stood out to you the most this week. What did you learn from this chapter that you can apply to your life?

2. ADAM AND EVE
Genesis 2

Unlike the rest of creation, human beings were not spoken into existence. We were made—by God's own hands. By creating woman *and* man, God satisfied the human need for relationships. And God has been doing that ever since.

We are given fathers and mothers, brothers and sisters, friends and partners, husbands and wives. These relationships bring joy and sorrow to our lives, but in them we grow to become what we never could become alone.

Genesis 2 also introduces us to one of life's greatest mysteries—the power of human choice. God introduces this power by planting a tree in the garden and telling Adam not to eat from it. We might wonder why God would allow the possibility of humanity's wrong choice by putting that tree in the garden; but without that possibility, there would be no freedom. And that's the real message of Genesis 2.

Human beings were created by God to be free. Obedience is our choice.

ADAM AND EVE: GENESIS 2

Share

Warm-Up Qs

- Do you imagine God as a male or a female or both? How do you picture God?

- When was the last time you felt really lonely? What caused you to feel that way?

- How would the world be different if there were only men and no women? How about if there were only women and no men?

Observe

Observation Qs

- According to v. 7, how did God make man? What caused the man to become a living being?

- What was the man's purpose in the Garden of Eden according to v. 15? What specific instruction did God give the man in vv. 16-17?

- What did God notice about the man in v. 18? What did God decide to do?

- According to vv. 21-23, how did God make woman? How did the man respond? What was God's design for man and woman according to v. 24?

Think

Interpretation Qs

- How does this creation account differ from the creation that happens in Genesis 1? What are the similarities?

- Why do you suppose the Bible records both Genesis 1 and 2? What does chapter 2 offer that chapter 1 doesn't include?

- Do you suppose it was significant that the woman was created out of man's rib? (v. 21) Why do you suppose God did that rather than creating her separately out of the dust in the ground?

- Look back at Genesis 1:27. Do you believe God's image is found only in man—or in woman and man together? What does that tell you about God?

Apply
Application Qs

- Why do you suppose God said, "It is not good for the man to be alone"? Do you suppose you could survive without other people in your life? Why/why not?

- Why do you suppose people tend to picture God as a man? Do you believe it's possible that God has both male and female characteristics? Why/why not?

- What do you believe God's original intention was for the relationship between women and men? Do you believe that our culture is following God's intention? (see v. 24)

- Why do you suppose God gave the possibility of choice by placing the tree of the knowledge of good and evil in the garden? What would human beings be like if we couldn't choose wrong?

Do
Optional Activity

Get play dough or clay and distribute an equal amount to each student in your group. Give them 10 minutes to form their clay into the shape of people. Debrief the experience by talking about the challenges they had with this exercise, and what it must have been like for God to shape a human being from the dust. Have everyone vote on the clay model that best represents God's design in Genesis 2.

QUIET TIME REFLECTIONS

Day 1: Genesis 2:1-3

- What word or verse stands out to you from these verses? Why?

- What did God do after creating the earth? What does that tell you about our own lives?

- Spend time today thinking about the ways you rest. Do you believe you need to work more—or rest more?

Day 2: Genesis 2:4-7

- What word or verse stands out to you from these verses? Why?

- How did God form the first man? What caused man to become a living being? How does that relate to our own lives?

- Spend time today thinking about the gift of breathing. Have you ever been thankful for being able to breathe?

Day 3: Genesis 2:8-14

- What word or verse stands out to you from this passage? Why?

- What two trees were in the Garden of Eden? Why do you suppose God put the tree of the knowledge of good and evil in the garden?

- Spend time today thinking about how God brought freedom of choice into the world.

Day 4: Genesis 2:15-17

- What word or verse stands out to you from these verses? Why?

- What does God command the man to do? Do you feel as though God is being unfair to the man by creating something he's supposed to avoid?

- Spend time today thinking about how God strengthens us by giving us choices.

Day 5: Genesis 2:18-22

- What word or verse stands out to you from this passage? Why?

- Why did God form the first woman? What does this tell you about God's intention for women and men?

- Spend time today thinking about the differences between men and women and why God created both.

Day 6: Genesis 2:23-25

- What word or verse stands out to you from these verses? Why?

- How do the man and woman feel about themselves by the end of this chapter? How does this differ from the way we feel today?

- Spend time today thinking about God's intention for man and woman and how things are different today.

Day 7: Genesis 2

Read through the whole chapter and write out the verse or passage that stood out to you the most this week. What did you learn from this chapter that you can apply to your life?

3. THE FALL
Genesis 3

"Did God really say . . . ?" Those same words echo in our brains when we think about disobeying God. The serpent poses the question to make God come across as the Grand Depriver. "Did God really say you're not supposed to eat from ANY tree in the garden?" The question is a disguised lie, because God doesn't say it exactly like that. (Genesis 2:16-17)

If Eve had stayed focused on the freedom she and Adam had, rather than the restraint placed on them—she might have responded differently. But the serpent was relentless. Temptation always is.

The serpent makes it sound like God's motive is to hold back goodness from Adam and Eve by restraining them. This is a strategy the devil still uses—dangling immediate pleasures before us to cause us to question God's restraints. But immediate pleasure often brings long-term pain—and sometimes we have to withstand immediate pain to secure long-term pleasure.

Adam and Eve ate from the tree of the knowledge of good and evil, deciding the taste of the fruit was worth the risk.

I wonder if they'd still make that choice.

THE FALL: GENESIS 3

Share

Warm-Up Qs

- When you think of the word *temptation*, what comes to your mind first?

- Do you suppose it's human nature to want what we can't have? What are some examples of this?

- Do you believe God is a "cosmic killjoy" who keeps us from having fun? Why/why not?

Observe

Observation Qs

- What question does the serpent ask Eve in v. 1? What do you notice about the wording of the question?

- Does Eve repeat God's exact command back to the serpent in v. 3? Compare her words with God's original command in Genesis 2:16-17.

- What does Adam say when God confronts him about eating from the tree in v. 12? What do you notice about the way Adam words his response?

- What are the consequences of Adam and Eve's choice? (See vv. 16-19.) What's altered from God's original intention for Adam and Eve? (vv. 21-24)

Think

Interpretation Qs

- Why do you suppose the serpent focused on the one thing Eve wasn't allowed to do? (v. 1) What effect did this have on Eve?

- What happened to Adam and Eve's relationship with God and each other after they ate from the tree? (vv. 10-12) Do you believe it brought them together—or separated them? Why?

- In what way do you see the consequences of Adam and Eve's sin played out in our lives? (see vv. 15, 16, and 19) Do you believe it was Adam and Eve's fault that sin came into the world—would a different couple have made a different choice? Would any other couple have made the same choice?

- Why does God utter the statement in v. 22? Do you believe this was what brought death (and the need for Christ) into the world?

Apply

Application Qs

- List all the mistakes Eve made just before she gave in to sin (vv. 2-6). If you were Eve, what would you have done differently to avoid eating from the tree?

- What temptations today are difficult to resist? Are there things our culture (or people around us) says are fine, but that God says are not? What can we learn from this chapter about listening to (and trusting) God?

- When you give in to sin, how do you feel? Satisfied—or guilty? Have you ever experienced short-term pleasure that led to long-term pain? If so, when?

- Is there a temptation in your life that you need support in combating? Are you willing to share it with your small group so they can pray for you and hold you accountable?

Do

Optional Activity

Have your group come up with a Top-10 Temptations list and write them down. Read them David Letterman-style (starting with #10 and working backward), and have your group vote (by clapping) for the top temptation. Afterward cut the paper so you have 10 pieces—one temptation on each—fold them, and put them in a basket. Have your group members each draw one piece of paper from the basket and write down a lie that accompanies that temptation (what it promises but doesn't deliver). Share these with the group.

QUIET TIME REFLECTIONS

Day 1: Genesis 3:1-3

- What word or verse stands out to you from these verses? Why?

- How does the serpent make it sound as though God is restricting Adam and Eve? Have you ever felt like God was restricting you?

- Spend time today thinking about why God puts boundaries in our lives. What would your life be like if you did everything you wanted to do?

Day 2: Genesis 3:4-7

- What word or verse stands out to you from these verses? Why?

- What caused Eve to give in to the temptation? What temptations do you struggle with the most?

- Spend time today thinking about your temptations and how you feel when you give in to them.

Day 3: Genesis 3:8-13

- What word or verse stands out to you from this passage? Why?

- How did Adam and Eve's disobedience affect their relationship with God? Did they take ownership over their actions? Why/why not?

- Spend time today thinking about how your disobedience affects your relationship with God. Do you ever try to hide from God?

Day 4: Genesis 3:14-16

- What word or verse stands out to you from these verses? Why?

- What are the consequences of the Fall for women? How do these consequences affect the relationship between women and men?

- Spend time today thinking about how the Fall affects the relationship between women and men and how you see these consequences lived out.

Day 5: Genesis 3:17-20

- What word or verse stands out to you from these verses? Why?

- What are the consequences of the Fall for men? Where in this passage do you see how death entered the world?

- Spend time today thinking about how our choices affect what happens to us.

Day 6: Genesis 3:21-24

- What word or verse stands out to you from these verses? Why?

- How do you see God taking care of Adam and Eve even after they sinned? What does that tell you about God?

- Spend time today thinking about God's grace, and how God loves us in spite of our imperfections.

Day 7: Genesis 3

Read through the whole chapter and write out the verse or passage that stood out to you the most this week. What did you learn from this chapter that you can apply to your life?

4. CAIN AND ABEL
Genesis 4

Genesis 4 tells the story of the first murder—and it's impossible to count how many have taken place since. The choices people make and the actions they take show the great risk God took by giving humans free will. This story illustrates that risk.

Adam and Eve give birth to two boys—Cain and Abel. The time comes for them to offer a sacrifice to God, and Cain's sacrifice was second best. But instead of focusing his attention on making a better sacrifice, Cain focuses his attention on his brother. And he lets jealousy get the best of him.

We may have freedom to treat people the way we want, but there are consequences for treating them badly. And those consequences extend beyond us. Because of Cain's actions, Adam and Eve lost a son—Abel. And even though Cain lived, he did so with the guilt and separation that came from his choice.

And that makes you wonder if Cain's loss wasn't the biggest of all.

CAIN AND ABEL: GENESIS 4

Share

Warm-Up Qs

- Do you ever feel "compared" to your brother or sister? If so, do you usually come out ahead or behind?

- Think of a time when you were really angry. How did you express your anger? Have you regretted how you expressed anger?

- Have you ever been jealous of someone who did something better than you? How did you handle it?

Observe

Observation Qs

- Look at vv. 3-4. What do you observe about the difference between Abel's offering and Cain's offering?

- What is God's warning to Cain in v. 7? What does God tell Cain to do?

- What is God's punishment for Cain in vv. 11-12? What is Cain's response? (vv. 13-14) How does God show grace in v. 15?

- What does God do for Adam and Eve in v. 25? What does the last verse say people started to do at this time?

Think

Interpretation Qs

- Why do you suppose God looked with favor upon Abel's sacrifice but not on Cain's? (vv. 4-5) What do you think would have made Cain's sacrifice more acceptable?

- How does God try to help Cain in vv. 6-7? Do you believe Cain regretted killing his brother—or do you believe he was glad about his actions? (see vv. 8-9)

- Look at Cain's response to God's punishment in v. 13-14. Do you believe Cain took responsibility for what he did? How do you see God's grace in v. 15? Do you suppose Cain deserved it?

- How do you see Cain's sin passed to his offspring? (see vv. 23-24) Do you believe this happens in families today? How does v. 26 reveal God's presence in the midst of dark times?

Apply

Application Qs

- When you think of the sacrifices you make for God, are you more like Abel (giving God your best) or Cain (giving God what's left)?

- Have you ever felt so jealous of someone that you wanted to hurt that person (through words or actions)? Without naming names, what did you do? What was the result?

- What do you tend to envy most in others—physical appearance, intelligence, athletic ability, or talent? Why?

- Is there someone you are envious of right now? What steps can you take to stop focusing on that person and start working on yourself?

Do

Optional Activity

Distribute pieces of paper to your students. Have them write down what they'd be willing to give up or do as a sacrifice to God. Go around the group and have your students rate each other's sacrifices with an A (like Abel) or a C (like Cain) or a B (in between Cain and Abel.). Have them give reasons for their ratings.

QUIET TIME REFLECTIONS

Day 1: Genesis 4:1-2

- What word or verse stands out to you from these verses? Why?

- Which of Adam and Eve's sons was born first? How does Eve give credit to God in regard to what she named him?

- Spend time today thinking about your name and whether it has any special meaning. Why did your parents name you what they did?

Day 2: Genesis 4:3-5

- What word or verse stands out to you from these verses? Why?

- Why does God favor Abel's sacrifice? Do you believe that was fair of God?

- Spend time today thinking about the sacrifices you make for God—and how God might feel about them.

Day 3: Genesis 4:6-8

- What word or verse stands out to you from these verses? Why?

- How does God give Cain a chance to make things right? What does Cain do with God's advice?

- Spend time today thinking about the times that you ignore God's voice in your life.

Day 4: Genesis 4:9-12

- What word or verse stands out to you from these verses? Why?

- How does God give Cain a chance to confess his sin? How does Cain respond?

- Spend time today thinking about how you approach God after you have sinned.

Day 5: Genesis 4:13-18

- What word or verse stands out to you from this passage? Why?

- How do you see God's grace to Cain again in this passage? What does that tell you about God's grace?

- Spend time today thinking about how God always gives us second chances, even when we experience the consequence of our own sin.

Day 6: Genesis 4:19-26

- What word or verse stands out to you from this passage? Why?

- How does God show grace to Adam and Eve for the sorrow they went through? What does this show you about God's compassion?

- Spend time today thinking about how God has shown compassion to you.

Day 7: Genesis 4

Read through the whole chapter and write out the verse or passage that stood out to you the most this week. What did you learn from this chapter that you can apply to your life?

5. THE FLOOD
Genesis 6-9

Noah is introduced as a righteous, blameless man who "walked faithfully with God."

Notice he's not described as standing with God. Or believing in God.

Noah walked with God.

His was a *movement* with the Almighty.

This implies more than a one-time decision; it's an everyday choice.

For Noah, the decision to walk with God led him on an amazing journey. God asked Noah to not trust what he sees, but to trust what he *doesn't see*. This is the first time in the Bible we encounter a human called to respond in faith.

Imagine if Noah sat on that ark with all those animals, and the rain never came. Noah would have been the biggest fool on the planet. But instead he and his family were the only ones left alive on earth. Noah's trust in God paid off.

From that point on, Noah knew by experience that what God says, God does.

And while Noah reaped the benefits of living by faith, he also saw the consequences of living without faith—and I bet those images stayed with him for the rest of his life.

THE FLOOD: GENESIS 6-9

Share
Warm-Up Qs

- Do you believe our basic nature is good or bad? Are we born sinners, or do we become sinners?

- What is the worst natural disaster you've ever experienced? How were you affected?

- Have you ever witnessed a miracle? If so, describe what happened. Do you believe miracles increase our faith in God?

Observe
Observation Qs

- Look at Genesis 6:5-7. How did God feel about the people he created? What did God decide to do in response?

- What did God ask Noah to do in Genesis 6:14-21? According to Genesis 7:17-24, how long did it rain? How long was the earth flooded?

- According to Genesis 8:6-12, how did Noah know that the water had receded? What did Noah do first after he left the ark? (v. 20)

- What did God promise Noah in Genesis 9:11? What is the symbol of the agreement establishing God's relationship with Noah? (vv. 9-11) What sign did God give Noah to symbolize his promise? (vv. 12-13)

Think
Interpretation Qs

- Look at how Genesis 6:9 describes Noah. What do you suppose it means that Noah "walked faithfully with God"? Is that the same as believing in God?

- What do you notice about Noah in Genesis 6:22 and Genesis 7:5? Of all the things Noah was asked to do in Genesis 6:14-21, which do you suppose was the most challenging?

- Look at Genesis 8:1. What do you suppose it means that "God remembered Noah"? What did "remembering Noah" lead God to do? (vv. 2-5). How did Noah "remember" God in v. 20?

- Look at Genesis 9:8-17. How is a covenant different from a contract? Would things have been different if God established a contract with Noah instead of a covenant?

Apply

Application Qs

- On a scale of 1-10, do you believe God is more a God of judgment or a God of grace? (1 = all judgment; 10 = all grace) What evidence of judgment and/or grace do you see in these chapters?

- Would you describe yourself as one who walks with God? Why/why not?

- Have you ever remembered something in a manner that moved you to action? If so, can you describe it for the group?

- Why do you suppose Noah acted the way he did at the end of chapter 9? (See vv. 20-23.) What warning does this give us about ourselves? What does this tell you about God's love for us?

Do

Optional Activity

Rent the DVD of *Evan Almighty* and show it to your group. Afterward, draw as many parallels as you can between Evan and Noah. What are the similarities? What are the differences? Did the movie help you understand a little more of what Noah must have gone through?

QUIET TIME REFLECTIONS

Day 1: Genesis 6:9-22

- What word or verse stands out to you from this passage? Why?

- What do you observe about Noah's relationship with God in this passage? Why do you believe God chose him to build the ark?

- Spend time today thinking about your relationship with God, and how you would respond if God asked you to do something really big.

Day 2: Genesis 7:1-10

- What word or verse stands out to you from this passage? Why?

- What do you notice about Noah's response to God in this passage? Have you ever had an opportunity to act on your faith?

- Spend time today thinking about how Noah must have felt going into the ark before it started to rain. Do you think he had any doubts at that point?

Day 3: Genesis 7:11-24

- What word or verse stands out to you from this passage? Why?

- Can you picture what it would be like to experience rain for 40 straight days and nights? Have you ever experienced God's power through nature? If so, when?

- Spend time today thinking about how you see the power of God evident in the world around you.

Day 4: Genesis 8:1-14

- What word or verse stands out to you from this passage? Why?

- How long did the flood last? Do you believe Noah wondered if it would ever end? Have you ever had to wait a long time for God to do something?

- Spend time today thinking about what God does to our faith in times of waiting.

Day 5: Genesis 8:15-22

- What word or verse stands out to you from this passage? Why?

- What did Noah do first when he got off the ark? When something good happens to you, do you thank God first?

- Spend time today thinking about what you're grateful to God for.

Day 6: Genesis 9:1-17

- What word or verse stands out to you from this passage? Why?

- When was the last time you saw the symbol of God's covenant with Noah? When you see rainbows, do you remember God's promise?

- Spend time today thinking about God's faithfulness to his promises.

Day 7: Genesis 7-8

Reread the account of the flood and write the verse or passage that stood out to you the most this week. What did you learn from this story that you can apply to your life?

6. TOWER OF BABEL
Genesis 11

Genesis 11 describes a time when everyone in the world spoke the same language.

People came together to create and build, which was not a bad thing. What was bad was their motivation for doing it. Instead of doing it to glorify God, they did it to glorify themselves.

Human power can look pretty good—that is, until God's power lands next to it. The Tower of Babel must have been kind of humorous in a way: First people are building this huge tower, then suddenly they can't communicate. Someone asks for a brick and is handed a ladder. He turns to ask someone else, and that person gives him some tar. Imagine the frustration and chaos. In an instant, human power is squashed.

A greater power has taken control.

When human beings build and create, we somehow believe we control the world. But no matter how powerful our buildings, they can be destroyed. No matter how great our technologies and inventions, they'll soon be obsolete. The longer we live, the more we realize our power is limited. God's power always has the last word.

And sometimes God even takes away our words to prove it.

TOWER OF BABEL: GENESIS 11

Share

- How many languages do you know? Are there any languages you wish you knew?

- Have you ever been in a country where you couldn't speak the language? If so, how did you communicate?

- How would the world be different if we all spoke the same language? Do you think it would be better or worse?

Observe

Observation Qs

- Look at v. 4. What did the people decide to do? According to this verse, what was their motivation for doing it?

- According to v. 6, what was the Lord's concern about people building the tower? What did God think would happen to them?

- What did the Lord do to stop the people from building the tower? What happened to them?

- After the people were scattered, whose genealogy is followed in vv. 10-32? What person of significance came from this line of people in vv. 25-26?

Think

Interpretation Qs

- What effect did speaking the same language have on the people? (see vv. 1-4) Do you believe it was good for them or bad for them? Why?

- Why do you think the Lord reacted the way described in v. 6? Do you think God was being paranoid? Why/why not?

- In what way do you see (from this chapter) that language gives you power?

- What happened to the people when their language was confused? (v. 8) In what way does language bring unity or separation?

Apply

Application Qs

- Do you know people who don't speak English very well? If so, how does the language barrier impact your relationships? Do you feel closer or more distant because of the language barrier?

- Has there ever been a time when you've done something that "made a name" for yourself? If so, what was it? (e.g., sports, academic, art, etc.)

- What does this story teach us about power? Do you believe there are modern-day examples of the Tower of Babel? If so, what are they?

- What is one way you could use your time, talent, or resources to do something for God (instead of yourself)?

Do

Optional Activity

Find someone (preferably from your small group) who can speak another language. Then have your students try to have a conversation with this person using only English, while the person uses only the other language. Let the conversation go for three to five minutes and then debrief the experience. Was it humorous? Frustrating? How much did you understand?

QUIET TIME REFLECTIONS

Day 1: Genesis 11:1-4

- What word or verse stands out to you from these verses? Why?

- What was the motivation of the people building the tower? Have you ever wanted to "make a name for yourself" in some way?

- Spend time today thinking about how to glorify God instead of yourself.

Day 2: Genesis 11:5-6

- What word or phrase stands out to you from these verses? Why?

- Why do you believe God was concerned over what the people were doing? Do you think he was concerned about their abuse of power?

- Spend time today thinking about the difference between abusing your power and using your power for good.

Day 3: Genesis 11:7-8

- What word or phrase stands out to you from these verses? Why?

- What power does language have to unite or separate? How do you see that in the world today?

- Spend time today thinking about how important language is, and what language you might want to learn to become closer to people who don't speak English.

Day 4: Genesis 11:9

- What word or phrase stands out to you from this verse? Why?

- What word in our vocabulary is associated with the Tower of Babel? How does it relate to this story?

- Spend time today thinking about how many languages and dialects exist, and where those languages are spoken. Which countries speak English?

Day 5: Genesis 11:10-26

- What word or phrase stands out to you from this passage? Why?

- Which of Noah's sons has his lineage traced in these verses? Do you see God's plan through Abraham beginning in this lineage? What connection do you see between the Shemites (Semites) and the Jews?

- Spend time today thinking about your lineage. What is your cultural background? When did your relatives first come to this country?

Day 6: Genesis 11:27-32

- What word or phrase stands out to you from this passage? Why?

- What facts do you pick up about Abram and Sarai in this passage that will be important for the future?

- Spend time today thinking about how big God's plan is, and how God is doing things now that we will understand later.

Day 7: Genesis 11

Reread the account of the tower of Babel and write out the verse or passage that stood out to you the most this week. What did you learn from this story that you can apply to your life?

7. THE CALL OF ABRAM
Genesis 12-15

The first we hear of Abram, God commands him to leave his country, his people, and his household.

And the amazing thing was . . . he went!

For Abram that meant leaving behind a life he knew for a life he knew nothing about. But he knew enough about God to take that risk. Do you?

When we're called to follow God, we're called to leave our old lives behind. In Abram's case, this meant a physical, literal leaving—traveling to a new, unknown place. God may or may not have the same thing in mind for us. Instead of a move out of the country, it could mean a move out of a relationship. Or it could be a move that sets you apart. And it may not be a physical move, but a spiritual move. And sometimes that's the biggest move of all. Because it doesn't just change your geography—it changes you.

As we read on, we see that Abram didn't always respond with faith. There were times when he responded with fear. But when that happened, God stayed with Abram. And Abram stayed with God. That's what it means to live the journey of faith.

THE CALL OF ABRAM: GENESIS 12-15

Share

Warm-Up Qs

- Have you ever moved somewhere? If so, how did you feel? (Excited? Nervous? Sad?) What was the hardest part about the move?

- On a scale of 1-10 (1 = nowhere, 10 = anywhere), how far are you willing to go with God?

- What in your life would be the hardest for you to let go of? (It can be a person, place, or thing.) Why?

Observe

Observation Qs

- Read Genesis 12:1-3. What did the Lord tell Abram to leave? Where did the Lord tell Abram to go? What did the Lord say would happen to Abram when he left?

- What did Abram tell his wife to say to the Egyptians? (See vv. 11-13.) Why? What ended up happening because of this? (See vv. 17-20.)

- Read Genesis 13:14-17. What does the Lord say to Abram about the land after he got there? What does the Lord say about Abram's offspring?

- Read Genesis 15:1-6. What is Abram's complaint to God in v. 2? What is the Lord's answer? (See v. 4.) How does Abram respond? (v. 6)

Think

Interpretation Qs

- What evidence of Abram's faith do you see in Genesis 12:4?

- How do you see Abram's faith falter in vv. 11-13? How do you suppose Abram felt when Pharaoh said what he did in vv. 18-19?

- What is inferred in Genesis 13:15-16 about Abram's offspring? What does this mean given that Abram was childless at this point?

- According to Genesis 15:6, how did Abram show his righteousness? Do you think righteousness has more to do with faith or works? Why?

Apply

Application Qs

- If God told you to leave everything you know for an unknown place, would you be able to do it? Why/why not?

- Do you find it easy or hard to trust God? Has anything happened in your life that makes you question God's faithfulness?

- What do you suppose is the connection between faith and righteousness? Do you consider yourself a faithful person? How about a righteous person?

- After reading about Abram's faith journey, would you say you have less faith, equal faith, or more faith than Abram? What could you (or God) do to increase your faith?

Do

Optional Activity

Blindfold half your students and have the other half serve as guides. Pair them off, and have the guides lead the blindfolded students around the room (or house). The more challenging the course, the better. If you have time, switch the blindfolds and let the other students serve as guides. Debrief the experience by asking the blindfolded students what role the guides played in giving them the confidence to move.

QUIET TIME REFLECTIONS

Day 1: Genesis 12:1-5

- What word or verse stands out to you from this passage? Why?

- Why do you suppose Abram was able to do what the Lord told him to do? What does that tell you about his relationship with God?

- Spend time today thinking about whether or not you do what God asks you to do. Is God asking anything of you right now?

Day 2: Genesis 12:10-20

- What word or verse stands out to you from this passage? Why?

- What happened to Abram's faith in this passage? How did God show him that lying was wrong?

- Spend time today thinking about how God lets you know when you've done something wrong.

Day 3: Genesis 13

- What word or verse stands out to you from this chapter? Why?

- How does Abram show his faith by letting Lot choose his land first? How does God reward him?

- Spend time today thinking about how you can trust God no matter what other people do—or what your circumstances are.

Day 4: Genesis 14:14-24

- What word or verse stands out to you from this passage? Why?

- How does Abram show his loyalty to Lot in this passage? Which of your family members is the most challenging for you to love? How does this passage inspire you?

- Spend time today thinking about how to love the people God has placed in your life—even when they aren't making the best choices.

Day 5: Genesis 15:1-6

- What word or verse stands out to you from this passage? Why?

- What obstacles were in the way of Abram believing the promise God gave him? What obstacles are in the way of you having total and complete faith in God?

- Spend time today thinking about how you can trust God more.

Day 6: Genesis 15:7-15

- What word or verse stands out to you from this passage? Why?

- What is the second promise God gives Abram in this passage? Have you ever felt like God was communicating to you through a dream?

- Spend time today thinking about the ways God communicates to you.

Day 7: Genesis 12

Reread Genesis 12 and write out the verse or passage that stood out to you the most from this chapter. What did you learn from this story that you can apply to your life?

8. HAGAR AND ISHMAEL
Genesis 16

Sometimes we have the patience to wait for God's plan. This chapter shows what can happen when we don't.

Sarai felt (with good reason) that she had waited long enough. Instead of staying on God's timeline, she tries to bring God on her timeline. What started out as a solution ended up creating more problems. This is what usually happens when we take over God's plan.

The good news is that even when we do take the wheel and crash the car, God *still* doesn't give up. We may step out of God's plan, but God works it into a bigger plan—and the original plan is not lost. That's what happens in this chapter.

Sarai couldn't have known the problems her impatience would create. The birth of Ishmael was the birth of the Arab people—and Arabs and Israelis have been in conflict ever since. Some scholars say it all began in this chapter: One woman taking God's job into her hands.

But in the end God showed Sarai who's in charge. And she eventually saw just how powerful God is.

HAGAR AND ISHMAEL: GENESIS 16
Share
Warm-Up Qs

- Do you consider yourself a patient person? Why/why not?

- What is the longest you can remember waiting for something you wanted? Is there anything you are waiting for now?

- Have you ever manipulated your circumstances to get something you wanted—and then regretted it later?

Observe

- Read vv. 1-2. What did Sarai say to Abram about the Lord? What did she suggest as an alternate plan?

- Look at vv. 3-5. Who was the instigator of Hagar and Abram coming together? What happened? (v. 4). How did Sarai react to the news?

- Who did Sarai blame for her suffering? (v. 5). How did Abram respond? (v. 6) What happened to Hagar?

- How did the Lord take care of Hagar in vv. 6-10? What name did Hagar give God in v. 13?

Think

Interpretation Qs

- What is Sarai's thought progression leading up to her plan? Do you suppose her thoughts about God contributed to her decision?

- Why do you suppose Abram went along with Sarai's plan? Do you believe he doubted that God would bring him a child through Sarai? Why/why not?

- Why do you suppose Sarai blamed Abram for something she suggested? (v. 5) Was it Abram's, Sarai's, or both their faults?

- How do you suppose Hagar felt about God when all this happened to her? Do you believe Hagar felt close to God in her pain or far from God? Why?

Apply

Application Qs

- Can you relate to what Sarai did in this chapter? Have you ever tried to "help God" give you something you wanted?

- In trying to solve their problems, Abram and Sarai created more problems. Can you think of a time when this happened to you?

- What does this chapter show us about God when we mess up? Does God reject us—or continue to show us grace? Where in your life do you need God's grace right now?

- There are many lessons in this chapter—on waiting for God's timing, having faith that God will come through, and not trying to make things happen on your own. Which of these lessons do you need most right now?

Do

Optional Activity

Make a list of all the methods people use today to have children (i.e., adoption, in-vitro fertilization, surrogate mothers, sperm donors, conception). Decide as a group which of these you believe God approves of. Which (if any) are questionable? How much should we take advantage of today's technology to do something we want when it isn't happening naturally? Does this compare to what Sarai did in this passage?

QUIET TIME REFLECTIONS

Day 1: Genesis 16:1-2

- What word or phrase stands out to you from these verses? Why?

- What motivated Sarai to do what she did? Can you relate to her at all?

- Spend time today thinking about times when you struggled to wait for God, and were tempted to do things on your own.

Day 2: Genesis 16:3-4

- What word or phrase stands out to you from these verses? Why?

- Why do you suppose Hagar was angry with Sarai after she got pregnant? Do you believe she may have felt used?

- Spend time today thinking about how you may have unintentionally hurt others trying to get your own way.

Day 3: Genesis 16:5-6

- What word or phrase stands out to you from these verses? Why?

- How did Sarai's actions affect her relationship with Abram? Who did Sarai blame?

- Spend time today thinking about the times you have blamed someone else for something you have done.

Day 4: Genesis 16:7-9

- What word or phrase stands out to you from these verses? Why?

- What do you notice about God's relationship to Hagar in these verses? How did God show Hagar she was not forgotten?

- Spend time today thinking about the ways God pursues us, even when we run away and feel lost.

Day 5: Genesis 16:10-12

- What word or phrase stands out to you from these verses? Why?

- How was Hagar's promise similar to Abram's promise? How was it different?

- Spend time today thinking about how God weaves our mistakes into a bigger plan.

Day 6: Genesis 16:13-16

- What word or phrase stands out to you from these verses? Why?

- What name did Hagar give to God? In what way do you experience God seeing you?

- Spend time today thinking about how God watches you and is with you all the time, no matter where you go or what you do!

Day 7: Genesis 16

Reread Genesis 16 and write out the verse or passage that stood out to you the most from this chapter. What did you learn from this story that you can apply to your life?

9. IS ANYTHING TOO HARD FOR GOD?
Genesis 17-18

We've read about *Abram* and *Sarai*—but in chapter 17, God changes their names to Abraham and Sarah, declaring that the couple will be the father and mother of many nations. And up to this point we've seen God's promise through Abram's eyes. But in chapter 18, we get to see it through Sarah's eyes.

Three visitors tell Abraham, now 99, that this time next year Sarah will have a son. In the past, this news would have brought hope. Now at 90, all Sarah can do is laugh. The visitor hears her and says to Abraham, "Why did Sarah laugh?" If I were Abraham I would have said, "Wouldn't you?"

It's at that point where Abraham and Sarah are met with one of my favorite verses. "Is anything too hard for the LORD?" (18:13) Their story will answer that question. But in the meantime, all they can do is laugh!

I believe God delights in doing the impossible. And the impossible often makes us laugh. At the age of most great-grandparents, Abraham and Sarah were about to become parents.

And the baby's name would forever symbolize their delight.

IS ANYTHING TOO HARD FOR GOD? GENESIS 17-18

Share

- If you could change your name, what name would you choose? Why?

- Is there anything in your life that feels impossible right now? If so, what?

- If you could ask for any miracle to increase your faith, what would it be?

Observe

Observation Qs

- How old was Abram when the Lord appeared to him in 17:1? What did the Lord say? What name did the Lord give him in v. 5?

- What name did God give Sarai in v. 15? What did God say about her in v. 16? How did Abraham respond?

- What did Abraham ask for Ishmael in v. 18? How did God respond? What did God say about the two sons in vv. 20-21?

- What do the three visitors say to Abraham in 18:10? How did Sarah respond in vv. 11-12? What do the visitors say in v. 14?

Think

Interpretation Qs

- Why do you suppose God gave Abraham a new name? (v. 5) Was there any significance in this?

- Why do you suppose God waited for Abraham to be 100 and Sarah to be 90 before God gave them a child? (vv. 15-17) What insight does this give us about God's timing?

- Why couldn't Ishmael be the promised son? (v. 18) How would that have altered God's plan?

- Look at Genesis 18:10-15. Do you believe God was angry with Sarah for laughing? Why/why not?

Apply

Application Qs

- In these chapters, God spoke to Abraham in different ways. What are some of the ways God has spoken to you? (Through the Bible? Another person? A conviction in your heart?)

- If God were to give you a new name based on a hope for your life, what would it be?

- What in your life right now feels "too hard," even for God? Where do you need to apply the words of Genesis 18:14?

- Do you have faith to believe God can do anything? Or do you believe there are some things God cannot do?

Do

Optional Activity

Google the Guinness Book of World Records for the oldest woman to give birth to a child. Who was it? Where did it happen? Did it happen naturally or by in-vitro fertilization? How many years difference between the Guinness record-holder and Sarah? How does this put into perspective what God did for Abraham and Sarah? (At the time of publishing, the oldest woman to give birth naturally was 59, and the oldest woman to give birth through in-vitro fertilization was 70.)

QUIET TIME REFLECTIONS

Day 1: Genesis 17:1-8

- What word or verse stands out to you from this passage? Why?

- Why did God change Abram's name to Abraham? How many times did God allude to Abraham's offspring in these verses? How do you suppose that made Abraham feel?

- Spend time today thinking about what a God-sized dream in your life would look like.

Day 2: Genesis 17:9-14

- What word or verse stands out to you from this passage? Why?

- What is the symbol of the covenant between God and Abraham's descendants? In what way do you see that covenant still being honored today?

- Spend time today thinking about God's covenant with the Jews—and how that covenant broadened to others through Jesus.

Day 3: Genesis 17:15-22

- What word or verse stands out to you from this passage? Why?

- Why do you believe God waited so long to deliver this promise to Abraham and Sarah? What does this tell you about how God develops our faith?

- Spend time today thinking about the unanswered prayers in your life, and how God might be developing your faith during this time of waiting.

Day 4: Genesis 17:23-27

- What word or verse stands out to you from this passage? Why?

- How do you see Abraham's heart as a father in this passage? What bond does he share with Ishmael on the same day God delivered the promise to him?

- Spend time today thinking about your relationship with your father. Is there any special bond you share? Are there any traditions you look forward to doing together?

Day 5: Genesis 18:1-8

- What word or verse stands out to you from this passage? Why?

- Do you suppose Abraham knew the visitors were from God? What are some clues in the passage that Abraham knew they were special?

- Spend time today thinking about what it would be like for an angel to visit you. Do you believe you'd recognize an angel if one came in human form?

Day 6: Genesis 18:9-15

- What word or verse stands out to you from this passage? Why?

- How was Sarah's response to the visitor's words similar to Abraham's response to God in Genesis 17:17? Do you believe Sarah's laugh was hopeful—or cynical?

- Spend time today thinking about what promise of God would make you laugh because you couldn't believe it.

Day 7: Genesis 17

Reread Genesis 17:1-22 and write out the verse or passage that stood out to you the most from this chapter. What did you learn from this story that you can apply to your life?

10. LEAVING EVIL BEHIND
Genesis 18-19

It's almost like a scene from a trashy movie. Two angels arrive to rescue Lot and his family. While they are inside Lot's house, the men of Sodom ask Lot if they can have sexual relations with them. It's a shocking scene, but it gives us a picture of how sinful Sodom had become. (To this day, homosexual acts are sometimes referred to as "sodomy.")

Because of Abraham's plea to save his nephew, the angels grab Lot, his wife and daughters, and instruct them to flee and not look back. But Lot's wife cannot do it. She turns her head, and her hesitation destroys her.

The more we turn toward our sins, the harder it is to leave them. In Lot's wife's case, it left her dead.

The chapter ends much like it begins—with a scene of desperation and disgust. Lot's daughters believe their only chance to bear children is with their own father. In a drunken stupor, Lot complies. It's a sad end to a sad life—and reveals what happens when we make our bed in sin.

Hopefully it's a lesson on not going down that same path.

LEAVING EVIL BEHIND: GENESIS 18-19

Share

Warm-Up Qs

- How would you define *evil*?

- Why do you suppose God allows evil in the world? Do you ever feel frustrated that God doesn't appear to intervene and do something about it?

- If you could put an end to any one form of evil (e.g., rape, child abuse, murder, human trafficking), which evil would you choose to stop? Why?

Observe

Observation Qs

- Read Genesis 18:20-33. What did Abraham say to "bargain" with God in vv. 24-33? What was the last number of people he asked God to spare in v. 32?

- What did the men of Sodom want to do with the angels who came to Lot's house? (19:5) What did Lot offer to do to appease them? (vv. 6-8)

- What did the angels do to the men of Sodom in v. 11? What did they tell Lot to do? (vv. 12-13) Who in Lot's family left with the angels, and who stayed behind? (vv. 14-16)

- What instructions did the men give to Lot's family? (v. 17). What happened to Sodom in vv. 24-25? What happened to Lot's wife? (v. 26)

Think

Interpretation Qs

- Do you believe God was being too lenient in saying he would not destroy Sodom for the sake of 10 people? (See Genesis 18:32.) Why/why not?

- Do you believe Lot was as evil as the men around him in Sodom? (See Genesis 19:2-8.) How do you suppose Lot and his family may have been affected by living in Sodom?

- Why do you suppose Lot hesitated fleeing Sodom in v. 16? Do you believe he would have stayed in Sodom if the angels hadn't grabbed his hand? Why/why not?

- Based on Genesis 18:30-36, do you believe Lot and his family learned their lesson after the destruction of Sodom? What does this tell you about the nature of sin?

Apply

Application Qs

- Do you ever wish God would do today what was done to Sodom? What do you wish God would destroy?

- How do you see God's grace displayed in this story? Do you believe God's judgment is stronger than God's grace—or vice versa?

- Is there a "place" that affects your life negatively? How does this chapter encourage you to stay away from that "place"?

- Do your friends have a good or bad influence on you? Is there anyone you need to spend less time with? Who would be good for you to spend more time with?

Do

Optional Activity

Sharks and Minnows game: Choose one person to be the shark, and put that person on one side of the room. The others will be minnows and stay on the other side of the room. Have the shark yell out categories such as "long hair," "brown hair," "under 5 feet 2 inches," "over 5 feet 2 inches," etc. You can make up categories ahead of time—best to choose things that will include more than one person. When the shark yells out the category, all minnows who fit the category will try to get to the other side of the room without the shark tagging them. If any of them get tagged, they become sharks, too. Keep playing until everyone becomes a shark. Debrief by asking, "When was it hardest to escape the shark? Can you draw any parallels between this game and what it's like to run away from sin?"

QUIET TIME REFLECTIONS

Day 1: Genesis 18:16-21

- What word or verse stands out to you from this passage? Why?

- Why did the Lord decide to show Abraham what was about to happen to Sodom? In what way does thinking about consequences keep us from sin?

- Spend time today thinking about the consequences of the sins that most tempt you.

Day 2: Genesis 18:22-25

- What word or verse stands out to you from these verses? Why?

- What argument does Abraham give God for what was about to happen? Do you ever consider it unfair that innocent people get punished for other people's sins?

- Spend time today thinking about the ripple effect of sin— how it not only affects the sinners but also people around them.

Day 3: Genesis 18:26-33

- What word or verse stands out to you from this passage? Why?

- Have you ever bargained with God about something? What does this passage show you about how God bargains with us?

- Spend time today thinking about how God wants us to have every opportunity to repent so we can experience God's grace.

Day 4: Genesis 19:1-11

- What word or verse stands out to you from this passage? Why?

- What do you think about Lot's depravity in this passage? Do you think he was aware of how bad his life had become?

- Spend time today thinking about how we become like the company we keep.

Day 5: Genesis 19:12-29

- What word or verse stands out to you from this passage? Why?

- Why do you think Lot hesitated to leave Sodom? Do you think it's hard to leave sin behind?

- Spend time today thinking about how we have to turn and run from our sins or we will continue to be stuck in them.

Day 6: Genesis 19:30-38

- What word or verse stands out to you from this passage? Why?

- In what way had life in Sodom influenced Lot's daughters? When it comes to values, how big an influence do parents have on their children?

- Spend time today thinking about the influence your parents have on you—and in what ways you want to be like them when you grow up.

Day 7: Genesis 18

Reread Genesis 18 and write out the verse or passage that stood out to you the most from this chapter. What did you learn from this story that you can apply to your life?

11. FEAR AND FAITH
Genesis 20-21

Sometimes our circumstances drive us to take control. Faith is about letting God take control instead. When we don't exercise faith, we not only miss out on seeing God's faithfulness, we miss out on being a witness to God's faithfulness. That's what happened to Abraham.

Abimelech never got to see Abraham's faith. Instead he was a victim of Abraham's lack of faith. It was the second time this happened to Abraham, but he still didn't get it. And for that reason, God will continue to work on Abraham's faith.

The journey of faith is about facing our fears—and letting God work through them. When we manage our own fears, we never get over them. And that's not how God wants us to live. When we're afraid to do something (that's not sinful, of course), there's a chance that's exactly what God wants us to do. When we do it, and God takes us through it, we'll know God in a deeper way. And that's God's ultimate goal for our lives.

Abraham may not have passed the test of faith this time, but with God, there will be another chance. There always is.

FEAR AND FAITH: GENESIS 20-21

Share

Warm-Up Qs

- Would you describe yourself as more fearful or faithful? Why?

- Why do you suppose it's important to God that we exercise faith?

- What's the biggest miracle you've experienced or observed?

Observe

Observation Qs

- Read Genesis 20:1-2. What does Abraham say about Sarah to Abimelech in vv. 1-2? What did Abimelech do?

- Read Genesis 20:3-10. What happened to Abimelech for taking Sarah home? (see v. 3) What did Abimelech tell God? (v. 4) How did God respond? (v. 6) What did Abimelech say to Abraham after he realized who Sarah was? (vv. 9-10)

- What was Abraham's reasoning for what he did? (See vv. 11-13.) How did Abraham make things right with Abimelech? (See vv. 17-18.)

- How did God finally fulfill his promise in Genesis 21:1-2? What was Abraham's son named? (v. 3) How did Sarah respond to all that happened in v. 4?

Think

Interpretation Qs

- Why do you believe it was hard for Abraham to trust God in Genesis 20? What was he afraid would happen?

- Do you believe Abimelech was a good king or a bad king based on his actions in vv. 3-9? Whose fault was it that he took Sarah?

- Look at Abraham's excuse in Genesis 20:11. Do you believe Abraham was relying on God or himself? How does Abraham rationalize his behavior in v. 12?

- What do you notice about the difference between Abraham's faithfulness in Genesis 20 and God's faithfulness in Genesis 21? How is God's faithfulness different than ours?

Apply
Application Qs

- Have you ever not spoken up about your faith because you were afraid of others' reactions? If so, describe what happened.

- When is it hardest for you to live out your faith? At home? At school? With your friends? On weekends?

- Is your relationship with God dependent on your faithfulness—or God's faithfulness? What's the difference? When you're not faithful, do you believe God stays with you or abandons you? (See 2 Timothy 2:13.)

- What is the hardest thing for you to trust God with right now? How can you make a step toward trusting God more this week?

Do
Optional Activity

Have your students list all the places they go during a week (e.g., home, school, friend's house, job, church, etc.). Then have them circle the places where people know they are Christians, and they're comfortable living out their faith in front of others. Then go around and discuss those places that they didn't circle—and why it's uncomfortable for them to live out their faith in those places. Spend some time praying for students to live for Christ in EVERY area of their lives.

QUIET TIME REFLECTIONS

Day 1: Genesis 20:1-5

- What word or verse stands out to you from this passage? Why?

- Can you relate to Abraham's repeat mistake of lying about Sarah? (See Genesis 12:13.) Is there any sin you struggle with repeatedly?

- Spend time today thinking about God's grace covering our sins—and the chances we're given over and over to overcome them.

Day 2: Genesis 20:6-13

- What word or verse stands out to you from this passage? Why?

- How does God show grace to Abraham in this passage? How does Abraham attempt to justify his mistake?

- Spend time today thinking about how we need to take ownership of our mistakes and confess them to God in order to receive forgiveness and healing.

Day 3: Genesis 20:14-18

- What word or verse stands out to you from this passage? Why?

- How do you see God's loyalty to Abraham in spite of his actions? What does that tell you about God's relationship with us—even when we sin?

- Spend time today thinking about God's unconditional love for you—no matter what you do.

Day 4: Genesis 21:1-7

- What word or verse stands out to you from this passage? Why?

- How do you suppose people responded when they found out Abraham and Sarah had a baby? In what way are our difficulties a testimony to God's power?

- Spend time today thinking about the hard things in your life that God might use to bring glory to himself and allow you to witness to God's power.

Day 5: Genesis 21:8-13

- What word or verse stands out to you from this passage? Why?

- Does God seem cruel to Hagar in this passage? Do you ever feel as though God is being cruel to you? If so, how?

- Spend time today thinking about how sometimes God's love and care may be painful to experience at first.

Day 6: Genesis 21:14-21

- What word or verse stands out to you from this passage? Why?

- How did God show love and compassion to Hagar and Ishmael? What does that tell you about how God works through our mistakes?

- Spend time today thinking about any mistakes you've made—and what God might do to redeem those mistakes so that good results.

Day 7: Genesis 21

Reread Genesis 21:1-20 and write out the verse or passage that stood out to you the most from this chapter. What did you learn from this story that you can apply to your life?

12. ABRAHAM'S TEST
Genesis 22

Nothing was more precious to Abraham than his son Isaac. For years Abraham prayed—and waited. Agonized—and waited. Cried out—and waited. And finally . . . Isaac had come. The joy Abraham felt! The laughter he and Sarah shared. The miracle they had witnessed. Until . . .

God told Abraham to take that son—his beloved son—and bind him to a donkey, take him up a mountain, and sacrifice him. Imagine the emotions that must have welled up inside of Abraham. How could God be asking this? We don't know Abraham's thoughts—but we do know his actions. "Early the next morning Abraham got up and loaded his donkey." (v. 3) No matter how he felt, Abraham obeyed. This chapter shows us how his faith had matured.

When Isaac asked him where the lamb was that they were sacrificing, Abraham replied, "God himself will provide." Abraham knew God would take care of it. Even if he wasn't sure how.

That is the definition of faith. God wants us to experience what faith can produce. The more we trust God, the more God can do in our lives.

Abraham's life proves it.

ABRAHAM'S TEST: GENESIS 22

Share

- Who/what in your life would be the hardest for you to lose? Why?

- Has God ever allowed something in your life that didn't make sense? If so, what was it?

- How important do you think it is that God is first in your life? Is God first right now?

Observe

Observation Qs

- What did God ask Abraham to do in Genesis 22:2? How did Abraham respond in v. 3?

- What did Abraham say to his servants in v. 5? What did Isaac ask him in v. 7? How did Abraham respond in v. 8?

- When did the angel intervene in Abraham's action? (See vv. 10-11.) What did the angel say in v. 12? What animal was provided for Abraham in v. 13?

- How did God reinforce his covenant to Abraham in vv. 15-18? Whom did God swear by? What did God say would be the result of Abraham's obedience in v. 18?

Think

Interpretation Qs

- How do you suppose Abraham felt about God when God asked him to sacrifice Isaac?

- Why do you suppose Abraham obeyed so quickly? (v. 3) What does that tell you about his faith? Why do you think Abraham was silent when he obeyed?

- When Isaac asked Abraham where the sacrifice was, why do you suppose Abraham answered the way he did? (v. 8) Do you believe Abraham was trying to hide his plan from Isaac—or is it possible Abraham believed God would provide a different sacrifice?

- Look at the angel's words in v. 16. Why do you suppose God gave Abraham this test? What do you think would've changed if Abraham had said no to God?

Apply

Application Qs

- If you were Abraham, would you have been willing to sacrifice Isaac? Why/why not?

- What has been the biggest loss in your life? How did it affect your relationship with God?

- Why do you believe it's important to God to give us tests of faith? Is it more for us or for God?

- What would be the hardest thing for you to sacrifice right now? Would you be willing to sacrifice it if God asked you to?

Do

Optional Activity

Have students each write on a piece of paper the one thing that would be hardest for them to sacrifice—and if it's something God wants them to actually give up or remove from their lives . . . or simply be willing to let go of. In an act of symbolism, have your students each fold their pieces of paper and hold it in their hands. Then have a time of prayer and invite students to open their hands if they're willing to give to God what's written on their piece of paper.

QUIET TIME REFLECTIONS

Day 1: Genesis 22:1-3

- What word or verse stands out to you from these verses? Why?

- What do you suppose was going on in Abraham's mind when God asked him to sacrifice Isaac? What would you have thought if you were in Abraham's position?

- Spend time today thinking about the greatest sacrifice you could give to God.

Day 2: Genesis 22:4-8

- What word or verse stands out to you from this passage? Why?

- How did Abraham show his faith to Isaac? In what sense was this important?

- Spend time today thinking about your witness to others: Can your family and friends see your faith in God?

Day 3: Genesis 22:9-12

- What word or verse stands out to you from these verses? Why?

- How had Abraham's faith evolved since telling the king that Sarah was his sister? How did his actions in this passage illustrate the strength of his faith?

- Spend time today thinking about how visible your faith is (through your actions).

Day 4: Genesis 22:13-14

- What word or phrase stands out to you from these verses? Why?

- How did God provide a sacrifice for Abraham? How was this like Jesus?

- Spend time today thinking about how God provided a substitute sacrifice for us in Jesus.

Day 5: Genesis 22:15-18

- What word or phrase stands out to you from these verses? Why?

- How was Abraham rewarded for putting God first in his life? Have you put God first?

- Spend time today thinking about anything that might be in the way of God being first in your life.

Day 6: Genesis 22:19-24

- What word or phrase stands out to you from these verses? Why?

- Why do you suppose this chapter ends with the mention of Abraham's family? Do you believe they're all part of the promise stated in v. 17?

- Spend time today thinking about your family—grandfathers, grandmothers, uncles, aunts, cousins, etc. Who among your extended family has a relationship with God?

Day 7: Genesis 22

Reread Genesis 22 and write out the verse or passage that stood out to you the most from this chapter. What did you learn from this story that you can apply to your life?

13. A PERFECT MATCH
Genesis 24

In this chapter, we see an example of faith's ripple effect. Abraham sent his servant to find Isaac a bride. The catch is, the servant is supposed to convince this bride-to-be to leave her home so he can bring her back to Isaac. The circumstances seem impossible. But Abraham knows the God of the impossible.

However, there's a problem: The servant has to make it happen.

The servant's first prayer asked God to make a bride appear for his master's sake. (vv. 12-14) When he opens his eyes, Rebekah is standing in front of him. The second prayer is no longer a third-person prayer: "The Lord has led me on the journey . . ." (v. 27) The prayer is now his own.

The amazing thing about this account is that the servant not only receives Abraham's faith—he passes it on. When he gets to Rebekah's house, he tells the story of his prayer and how God answered it. Rebekah's family responds with an affirmation of faith. (v. 50)

And by the end of the chapter, the servant returns with two things he didn't have when he started his journey:

A bride for Isaac.

And a faith for himself.

A PERFECT MATCH: GENESIS 24

Share
Warm-Up Qs

- What do you think is most important for couples to be a good match?

- What qualities are you looking for in the person you want to marry? What quality is most important to you?

- Have you ever been impressed or inspired by someone else's faith? Whose faith do you admire most?

Observe
Observation Qs

- What did Abraham ask his servant to do in vv. 3-4? What concerns did the servant have? (v. 5) What did Abraham insist in v. 6?

- How did the servant make his vow to Abraham? (v. 9) What did he do in vv. 12-14? What signs does he ask for?

- When did Rebekah appear to the servant? (v. 15) How was she related to Abraham? What signs did she give the servant that she was the woman he prayed for? (See vv. 14 and 19.)

- What did the servant do first after his encounter with Rebekah? (v. 26) After the servant explained the story to her relatives, what question did they ask Rebekah? (v. 58) What did she say?

Think
Interpretation Qs

- How did Abraham's faith compare/contrast with the servant's faith at the beginning of the chapter? (see vv. 5, 7)

- Do you believe Abraham's faith had an influence on the servant? (see vv. 9, 12) How did the servant's faith evolve in this chapter? (see vv. 26, 48)

- How did Rebekah show her faith in this chapter? (see especially v. 58) How did her actions affect the servant's confidence in God?

- How many things happened in this story to confirm that Rebekah was the match for Isaac? What do you believe confirmed it for Isaac? (see vv. 66-67)

Apply

Application Qs

- Have you ever been strengthened by someone else's faith? Whose faith has had the greatest impact on you?

- Have you ever helped someone become stronger in faith? Without naming names, what happened?

- In this chapter, the servant tells Laban the whole story of how God led him to Rebekah and answered his prayer. (vv. 34-49) How important is it to our faith to tell stories of God's faithfulness? When was the last time God was faithful to you?

- What qualities are you looking for in a mate? How important is it that a potential wife or husband has faith in God?

Do

Optional Activity

Have your students write down all the qualities they want in mates, then have them circle the most important qualities. Finally give each of them some time to write a prayer for the person God may one day give them as husband or wife. Encourage your students to continue praying for this unknown person, that God would reveal him/her at the right time, and that he/she will have the courage to trust God and wait.

QUIET TIME REFLECTIONS

Day 1: Genesis 24:1-9

- What word or verse stands out to you from this passage? Why?

- How does Abraham show his faith to his servant in this passage? How do you show your faith to others?

- Spend time today thinking about how you show your faith to the people in your life.

Day 2: Genesis 24:10-21

- What word or verse stands out to you from this passage? Why?

- How did the servant experience his first answer to prayer in this passage? When was the last time one of your prayers was answered?

- Spend time today thinking about how God delights in answering our prayers when we are seeking God's direction.

Day 3: Genesis 24:22-31

- What word or verse stands out to you from this passage? Why?

- How did the servant show his newfound faith in God for answering his prayers? What do you think it means to worship God?

- Spend time today thinking about the ways you can worship God every day.

Day 4: Genesis 24:32-50

- What word or verse stands out to you from this passage? Why?

- What effect did the servant's testimony have on Rebekah's family? How did they respond?

- Spend time today thinking about how much you reveal to others what God does in your life.

Day 5: Genesis 24:51-60

- What word or verse stands out to you from this passage? Why?

- Do you observe evidence of Rebekah's faith in this passage? Do you believe you would have gone if you were her?

- Spend time today thinking about what compels you to believe something is from God, and how you need to respond.

Day 6: Genesis 24:61-67

- What word or verse stands out to you from this passage? Why?

- In what way was God's will confirmed in Isaac and Rebekah's relationship? How do you believe this made the servant feel?

- Spend time today thinking about the person God may have for you to marry—and say a prayer for that person to grow in his/her relationship with God.

Day 7: Genesis 24

Reread Genesis 24 and write out the verse or passage that stood out to you the most from this chapter. What did you learn from this story that you can apply to your life?

14. TWINS OF PROPHECY
Genesis 25

From the start, Jacob was on Esau's heel. Literally.

Even as a baby, Jacob was trying to control his birth order. And he wouldn't give up until he did.

Rebekah started to feel Jacob's personality in her womb. The twins jostled inside her, and when Rebekah asked the Lord about it, the Lord gave Rebekah a prophecy. (v. 23) We can't say whether Jacob's personality was a result of the prophecy, or the prophecy was a result of Jacob's personality. But God foreknew what Jacob would be like.

Esau was also a part of the prophecy. His role as firstborn would be overturned. At first, it seemed unfair, but as Esau grew, it became clearer why: While Jacob was conniving, Esau was careless. And this chapter gives evidence of both.

Certainly Jacob took advantage of Esau's carelessness. But the bottom line is that Esau gave in. Neither of them knew God had sealed their fates before birth. They made their own choices. And those choices confirmed their fates.

Is life more God's will or our choices? This chapter answers the question.

Both.

TWINS OF PROPHECY: GENESIS 25

Share

Warm-Up Qs

- Do you believe we're more a product of our nature (personality) or nurture (environment, family circumstances)? Which has the most influence on how we turn out?

- Do you know any twins? If so, how are they alike? How are they different?

- Do you believe your life is controlled by God—or by you?

Observe

Observation Qs

- Why did Isaac pray for Rebekah in v. 21? What happened?

- What did Rebekah feel inside her womb? (v. 22) What did the Lord say about it? (v. 23)

- Which twin was born first? (v. 25) What was the second twin doing when he came out? (v. 26)

- What did Jacob ask for in exchange for giving Esau some stew? (v. 31) How did Esau respond? (vv. 32-33)

Think

Interpretation Qs

- Do you believe the Lord's prophecy (v. 23) dictated the way Jacob and Esau turned out—or did they have a choice?

- What does Jacob's birth show you about his personality? (v. 26) In what way was it symbolic of his life?

- Do you think the selling of the birthright was more Jacob's fault—or Esau's? (vv. 30-34) Why?

- Why do you suppose v. 34 says that "Esau despised his birthright"? Does that seem like a harsh statement—or a true statement? Why?

Apply

Application Qs

- Between Jacob and Esau, whose personality is more like yours? Why?

- Do you have a brother or sister who you feel competitive with? Do you usually come out ahead or behind?

- Do you believe you make your own decisions—or that God controls everything? What insights do you get from this chapter regarding this question?

- Do you tend to focus on others and what they have—or do you make the most of what you have? What are the gifts and talents God has given you?

Do

Optional Activity

Pass out paper to your students and have them write a "prophecy" about the person to their right, based on what they know about that person. Fold up the prophecies and put them in the middle of the group. Read each one out loud and have the group guess who the person is for each prophecy. Vote as a group regarding if the prophecy is/is not likely to happen.

QUIET TIME REFLECTIONS

Day 1: Genesis 25:1-11

- What word or verse stands out to you from this passage? Why?

- In spite of all the children Abraham had, who did he leave everything to when he died? Why do you think he did that?

- Spend time today thinking about how Isaac was Abraham's most-treasured son—yet he was willing to sacrifice him to put God first.

Day 2: Genesis 25:12-18

- What word or verse stands out to you from this passage? Why?

- Why do you suppose this passage about Ishmael's lineage is included in the Bible? What does it show about God's heart for all people?

- Spend time today thinking about how God includes everyone—even people who might feel as though their lives are mistakes.

Day 3: Genesis 25:19-21

- What word or verse stands out to you from these verses? Why?

- How is Rebekah's story (of becoming a mother) similar to Sarah's? How is it different?

- Spend time today thinking about how God gives and withholds—and how we need to trust God's timing with everything.

Day 4: Genesis 25:22-23

- What word or phrase stands out to you from these verses? Why?

- How much of our life is decided before we are born? How does this passage make you feel about your own life?

- Spend time today thinking about the life God has for you—what part is determined by your choices, and what part is predetermined by God.

Day 5: Genesis 25:24-26

- What word or phrase stands out to you from these verses? Why?

- How was the birth of Jacob and Esau already a fulfillment of the prophecy that was given to them?

- Spend time today thinking about how much of your personality was already in place when you were born. Can you see your uniqueness when you compare yourself to your siblings?

Day 6: Genesis 25:27-34

- What word or phrase stands out to you from this passage? Why?

- Who do you think was more wrong in this passage—Jacob or Esau? Why?

- Spend time today thinking about how important it is to not "sell out" on who you're meant to be. Do you feel as though you're living out God's dream for you?

Day 7: Genesis 25

Reread Genesis 25 and write out the verse or passage that stood out to you the most from this chapter. What did you learn from this story that you can apply to your life?

15. JACOB'S BLESSING
Genesis 27

Imperfect people are used to accomplish God's purposes. This story shows us how.

Rebekah had received God's prophecy many years ago, and she knew Isaac was ready to give his blessing. So she intervened and put Jacob in Esau's place. She probably felt she was fulfilling God's will, but the way she went about it was questionable—at best.

Jacob is a bit more innocent than Rebekah in this chapter. But Jacob is a prime player in the deceit. He wasn't concerned about his brother's feelings. His only concern was that he might get caught. (v. 12) Jacob may have felt justified in his actions because Esau had already sold him his birthright. But Jacob's motives were mixed—at best.

Esau looks like the victim in this story. But a closer look helps you see his poor character. By giving his birthright to Jacob for some soup, Esau revealed how little he cared for it. Then he cried when it was taken away. If Esau had a stronger character, perhaps the prophecy would have been different. But he was weak and vulnerable—at best.

And so the prophecy was fulfilled.

But its fulfillment was messy—at best.

JACOB'S BLESSING: GENESIS 27

Share

Warm-Up Qs

- Do you believe God knows all the decisions you'll ever make before you make them? Why/why not?

- What is the greatest gift you've ever received? When did you receive it and from whom?

- Have you ever had a brother or sister receive a gift you wanted? If so, how did it feel?

Observe

Observation Qs

- What did Rebekah do after she heard Isaac speak to Esau about the blessing? (vv. 5-10) What did she tell Jacob to do?

- What was Jacob worried about in vv. 11-12? How did his mother respond? (v. 13)

- How many times did Jacob lie to Isaac about who he was? (see vv. 19, 24) What ultimately caused Isaac to give Jacob his blessing? (vv. 26-27)

- How did Isaac respond when he found out he had been deceived? (v. 33) What did Esau say when he found out Jacob got his blessing? (v. 34)

Think

Interpretation Qs

- Do you agree that Jacob and Rebekah should have done what they did to get Isaac's blessing? Why/why not?

- Do you believe Esau played any part in Jacob getting his blessing—or was he totally innocent? (Remember Genesis 26:32-34.)

- Who was the greatest deceiver in this chapter—Rebekah or Jacob? Why?

- Do you believe that God knew everything that would happen in this chapter? If so, do you believe God approved of it?

Apply

Application Qs

- Are we responsible for our actions if God knows beforehand what we're going to do? Why/why not?

- Do you believe it's possible to make a decision that's outside God's will? In what way do our decisions affect/not affect God's ultimate control?

- Have you ever had a prophecy come true in your life or someone else's life? If so, what was it?

- Is there any desire that you're tempted to "help" God fulfill in your life? How does the fallout from this chapter encourage you to wait for God to work?

Do

Optional Activity

Go around the group and have your students share one dream they have for their lives. Have them think of the things they can do to help make their dreams come true—and what things they need to leave up to God. Have them write down one thing they will do—and one thing they won't do—to make their dreams come true. Lead them in a prayer to trust their dreams to God.

QUIET TIME REFLECTIONS

Day 1: Genesis 27:1-10

- What word or verse stands out to you from this passage? Why?

- How did Rebekah try to "help God" in this passage? Have you ever done that?

- Spend time today thinking about what it means to "let go and let God."

Day 2: Genesis 27:11-17

- What word or verse stands out to you from this passage? Why?

- Who is more responsible for the deception in this passage—Rebekah or Jacob?

- Spend time today thinking about what kind of influence your mother has over you.

Day 3: Genesis 27:18-24

- What word or verse stands out to you from this passage? Why?

- How many times did Jacob lie in this passage? Do you believe it was hard for Jacob to deceive his father?

- Spend time today thinking about the last time you lied (or withheld something you should have shared). How did you feel afterward?

Day 4: Genesis 27:25-29

- What word or verse stands out to you from this passage? Why?

- What does Isaac's blessing say about Jacob's relationship with Esau? How did this fulfill the prophecy in Genesis 25:23?

- Spend time today thinking about how God knows the future—including decisions that haven't been made.

Day 5: Genesis 27:30-40

- What word or verse stands out to you from this passage? Why?

- Do you believe Esau is an innocent victim—or a victim of his own negligence?

- Spend time today thinking about how to protect and preserve the things that are important to you.

Day 6: Genesis 27:41-46

- What word or verse stands out to you from this passage? Why?

- What price did Jacob pay for his deception? Do you believe it was worth it?

- Spend time today thinking about how deception can affect relationships.

Day 7: Genesis 27

Reread Genesis 27 and write out the verse or passage that stood out to you the most from this chapter. What did you learn from this story that you can apply to your life?

16. LEAH AND RACHEL
Genesis 29-30

Both of Jacob's wives experienced loss and heartbreak. But God didn't forget either of them. Leah watched her sister have her husband's heart. Rachel watched her sister have her husband's sons. And God observed both of their pain.

While Leah had to bargain for Jacob's affection (30:15), Rachel had to bargain for Jacob's seed (30:1). Leah never had as much love, and Rachel never had as many children—but both had a measure of God's blessing. This illustrates how God works in our lives.

Life is filled with blessings and challenges, and God wants us to learn to live with both. In Philippians 4:12, Paul writes that he's learned "the secret of being content in any and every situation, whether well fed or hungry, whether living in plenty or in want." Will we focus on the things we don't have—or look at the things we do have?

God gives us the choice. Our lives give us the opportunity.

LEAH AND RACHEL: GENESIS 29-30

Share

Warm-Up Qs

- Do you tend to focus on your blessings or your challenges? Why?

- If you had to choose between being loved and having children, which would you choose?

- If you could trade places with someone, who would it be and why?

Observe

Observation Qs

- Look at Genesis 29:16-18. How are Leah and Rachel described? Which one was Jacob in love with? How long did he agree to work for her?

- How did Laban deceive Jacob in Genesis 29:22-26? How many more years did he have to work for Rachel? (v. 27) How many women did he end up with?

- What did the Lord do for Leah in Genesis 29:31-35? How did Rachel respond to her sister's good fortune in Genesis 30:1? What did she say to Jacob?

- What finally happened to Rachel in Genesis 30:22? How many children did Jacob have altogether?

Think

Interpretation Qs

- How do you suppose Leah felt when her father gave her to Jacob? (Genesis 29:23-25) How do you suppose Rachel felt?

- In your opinion, who had the greatest challenge? Rachel or Leah? Who had the greatest blessing?

- How do you see God's provision in Rachel and Leah's lives? Where do you see God's grace in this story?

- Do you see Jacob as the innocent victim in this story? Or do you believe God might have allowed this experience to show Jacob what it felt like to be deceived? (Remember Genesis 27.)

Apply

Application Qs

- Has God ever allowed a difficulty in your life to make you a better, stronger person? If so, describe what happened.

- What circumstances in your life frustrate you right now? Can you think of any good that could come from them?

- Is there anyone in your life who has something you wish you had? If so, how has your "want" affected your relationship?

- How can Philippians 4:12 help you in your perspective?

Do

Optional Activity

Have your students each make a list of five good things in their lives (i.e., blessings) and five bad things in their lives (i.e., bummers). Then have them define each of the blessings/bummers using a 1-10 scale (1 = think about it all the time; 10 = don't think about it at all). Based on their lists, determine as a group if they focus more on their blessings or their bummers? Have them each make a commitment to begin every day thanking God for one blessing in their lives.

QUIET TIME REFLECTIONS

Day 1: Genesis 29:1-14

- What word or verse stands out to you from this passage? Why?

- How do you see God's hand in taking care of Jacob?

- Spend time today thinking about how God guides us—even when we face the unknown.

Day 2: Genesis 29:15-30

- What word or verse stands out to you from this passage? Why?

- How did Jacob suffer consequences because of his deception?

- Spend time today thinking about how God shapes and refines us through our circumstances.

Day 3: Genesis 29:31-35

- What word or verse stands out to you from this passage? Why?

- How do you see God's care for Leah in this passage?

- Spend time today thinking about how God sees our pain—and doesn't leave us in it alone.

Day 4: Genesis 30:1-13

- What word or verse stands out to you from this passage? Why?

- What did Rachel do to solve her pain of not being able to have a child? Do you think it was a good move?

- Spend time today thinking about what you do when you can't have something you want.

Day 5: Genesis 30:14-24

- What word or verse stands out to you from this passage? Why?

- How did Rachel eventually become pregnant? Was it her doing or God's?

- Spend time today thinking about how God is in control—and we can trust that no matter what our circumstances.

Day 6: Genesis 30:25-43

- What word or verse stands out to you from this passage? Why?

- How would you rate the relationship between Laban and Jacob? Do you suppose it was based on care or manipulation—or both?

- Spend time today thinking about the relationships in which you feel truly loved, without condition.

Day 7: Genesis 29

Reread Genesis 29 and write out the verse or passage that stood out to you the most from this chapter. What did you learn from this story that you can apply to your life?

17. WRESTLING WITH GOD
Genesis 32

Jacob was about to face Esau. He knew this would be the struggle of his life. He had deceived Esau, stolen his birthright, and they have not seen each other since. Jacob prepared for their meeting in his usual way—bribing him with gifts, then dividing his goods to protect himself. Then he calls on God to support him. (v. 11) But Jacob learns in this chapter that God is more than a support to Jacob's strategies—God is the one in control.

After Jacob sent his presents, his servants, and his family ahead of him, he is alone. An angel then appeared in the form of a man, and the two of them wrestled until daybreak. The angel started to leave, but Jacob grasped him, saying "I will not let you go unless you bless me." Jacob had spent his life trying to acquire blessings himself; now he realized who the true source of blessing is.

Jacob got his blessing—but he was also left with a wound. From this point on, Jacob's limp would remind him of his dependence on God.

Perhaps that was the blessing Jacob needed most.

WRESTLING WITH GOD: GENESIS 32

Share

Warm-Up Qs

- Have you ever "wrestled with God" about anything? If so, what was it?

- Do you believe that God really sent angels to earth? If so, do you believe God sends them today? If so, what do they look like?

- Have you ever prayed hard for God to bless you in some way or with something? If so, what did you ask for?

Observe

Observation Qs

- What did the messengers tell Jacob in v. 6? How did Jacob react? (v. 7) What did he do?

- What did Jacob pray in vv. 9-11? What promise from God did he claim in v. 12?

- What did Jacob send ahead of him before he met Esau? (v. 21) Who was Jacob with on the night before he met Esau? (v. 24) What did they do?

- What did Jacob tell the man in v. 26? What name did the man give Jacob in v. 28? What happened to Jacob after he wrestled with God? (v. 31)

Think

Interpretation Qs

- Why was Jacob afraid of Esau? (v. 7) Do you believe he was being paranoid or realistic in his fear?

- What does Jacob's prayer tell you about his faith? (vv. 9-12) Do you believe his faith was mature or immature? Why?

- What do you suppose Jacob's motives were for sending gifts to Esau? Did Jacob really feel bad and want to give him something, or did Jacob do it to protect himself?

- How did Jacob change after he wrestled with God? Do you believe he became stronger or weaker than before? Why?

Apply

Application Qs

- Has something hard ever happened in your life that matured your faith? How mature would you say your faith is now?

- Do you tend to pray for what you want or what God wants? How would your relationship with God change if you prayed more for what God wanted?

- What might God "break" in you if God were to wrestle with you? How would it change you?

- If God were to give you a new name that symbolized your relationship with Him, what would it be? What would you like it to be?

Do

Optional Activity

Pair off your group and have them arm wrestle. Then have the winners pair off and hold more arm-wrestling matches. Keep going until you find your arm-wrestling champ. Let that person be the first to choose a name for someone in the group—something that symbolizes the recipients' personality/relationship with God—and have the rest of the group guess who it is. Then that person will choose a name for someone else—and the group will guess who that is—and so on . . . until everyone has been given a new name. Keep these names as a code known only to your group.

QUIET TIME REFLECTIONS

Day 1: Genesis 32:1-5

- What word or phrase stands out to you from this passage? Why?

- How does Jacob take the initiative to make peace with Esau?

- Spend time today considering if there's anyone you need to make peace with—and if you need to take the initiative.

Day 2: Genesis 32:6-8

- What word or phrase stands out to you from these verses? Why?

- What did Jacob interpret from the messenger's report about Esau? Why did he assume Esau would attack him?

- Spend time today thinking about how our fears can keep us from taking risks to reconcile with others.

Day 3: Genesis 32:9-12

- What word or phrase stands out to you from these verses? Why?

- What promise did Jacob stand on in his prayer?

- Spend time today thinking about how you can stand on God's promises when you pray.

Day 4: Genesis 32:13-21

- What word or phrase stands out to you from this passage? Why?

- What plan did Jacob devise to pacify Esau? Do you believe he was relying on God?

- Spend time today thinking about how to lean on God's help instead of your own.

Day 5: Genesis 32:22-26

- What word or phrase stands out to you from this passage? Why?

- Do you suppose Jacob knew who he was wrestling with? Why/why not?

- Spend time today thinking about the times you've "wrestled with God."

Day 6: Genesis 32:27-32

- What word or phrase stands out to you from this passage? Why?

- What happened to Jacob as a result of wrestling with God? Did he "win" the wrestling match?

- Spend time today thinking about how God invites us to wrestle through issues with him so we can experience a real relationship with him.

Day 7: Genesis 32

Reread Genesis 32 and write out the verse or passage that stood out to you the most from this chapter. What did you learn from this story that you can apply to your life?

18. SURPRISED BY GRACE
Genesis 33

It had been 20 years since Jacob stole Esau's birthright, leaving Esau to pick up the pieces of a life he neither wanted nor deserved. Now Jacob and Esau were about to meet for the first time since. You can imagine how Jacob felt.

As Jacob approached Esau, he began bowing in humility and fear. Suddenly Esau broke into a sprint, threw his arms around Jacob, and kissed him. Esau welcomed Jacob with undeserved grace. And Jacob witnessed the presence of God. (v. 10)

We are never more like God than when we forgive people who don't deserve it. When we stay bitter, we're the ones who suffer—even if our bitterness is deserved. When we choose to forgive, even when others do not deserve it, we're the ones who are free.

Jacob stole Esau's blessing, but God took care of Esau. (v. 9) He doesn't need Jacob to pay him back. It's an example to us regarding what grace can do—not only in the lives of those we forgive, but in our own lives as well.

When we let God take care of injustice done to us, we can experience the surprise of grace.

SURPRISED BY GRACE: GENESIS 33

Share

Warm-Up Qs

- Have you ever been afraid to see someone because you were just in a fight? How did you handle it?

- When you're in trouble, do you ever try to do nice things to "lessen the blow" in your own life?

- Have you ever forgiven someone who didn't deserve it? Has someone else ever done that for you?

Observe

Observation Qs

- Who did Jacob put in front of the line as Esau approached? (v. 2) Who was next? Who was last?

- How did Jacob refer to himself in v. 5? What did Jacob's family do to Esau when they met him? (v. 7)

- Why did Jacob send gifts ahead to Esau? (v. 8) How did Esau respond? (v. 9) Why did Esau end up keeping the gifts? (v. 11)

- What did Jacob say about Esau in v. 10? How did Jacob refer to himself and Esau in vv. 13-15?

Think

Interpretation Qs

- Why do you suppose Jacob put his family in the order he did in v. 2?

- What did Esau's response to Jacob tell you about his character? How had Esau changed from when Jacob last saw him in Genesis 27?

- Why do you suppose Jacob stated that seeing Esau's face was like seeing the face of God? (v. 10)

- Do you believe Jacob was truly repentant of how he treated Esau? Or was he just bribing him out of self-protection?

Apply

Application Qs

- How would you have felt toward Jacob if you were Esau? Could you have responded the way Esau did? If so, what would you have done? If not, why not?

- Is there anyone in your life you feel any resentment toward? How have you handled it?

- How does this chapter encourage you regarding those who've hurt you? What can you learn from Esau?

- Is there someone in your life you need to forgive? If so, will you be able to?

Do

Optional Activity

Rent *Les Miserables*. Show the scene in which Jean Valjean takes the silver from the priest and gets caught, and the priest tells the authorities he gave the silver to Valjean. Ask students if they've ever experienced undeserved grace like that, and if so, what effect it's had in their lives.

QUIET TIME REFLECTIONS

Day 1: Genesis 33:1-3

- What word or phrase stands out to you from these verses? Why?

- What does the order of Jacob's procession tell you about his relationships?

- Spend time today thinking about how you would position your loved ones if you were marching into a scary place? Would you, like Jacob, be willing to be in the front?

Day 2: Genesis 33:4-5

- What word or phrase stands out to you from these verses? Why?

- How did Esau exemplify God's grace in these verses? Have you ever been able to forget a wrongdoing like Esau did?

- Spend time today thinking about who in your life you need to forgive right now.

Day 3: Genesis 33:6-9

- What word or phrase stands out to you from these verses? Why?

- What is the surprise in these verses? Do you believe the surprise was different from what Jacob expected?

- Spend time today thinking about a time when someone surprised you with grace (e.g., when you were expecting anger or punishment and received forgiveness and kindness instead).

Day 4: Genesis 33:10-11

- What word or phrase stands out to you from these verses? Why?

- What did Jacob say Esau's face is like? Why do you suppose Jacob said this?

- Spend time today thinking about when you've seen the face of God in others.

Day 5: Genesis 33:12-15

- What word or phrase stands out to you from these verses? Why?

- In what way do you see the relationship between Jacob and Esau as transformed in these verses? How is their relationship different from what it was in Genesis 27?

- Spend time today thinking about a relationship of yours that needs transformation by the grace of God.

Day 6: Genesis 33:16-20

- What word or phrase stands out to you from this passage? Why?

- What did Jacob do when he arrived at the city of Shechem? Why do you suppose he stopped to worship God?

- Spend time today thinking about whether or not you express gratefulness to God after God answers your prayers.

Day 7: Genesis 33

Reread Genesis 33 and write out the verse or passage that stood out to you the most from this chapter. What did you learn from this story that you can apply to your life?

19. RESULTS OF REVENGE
Genesis 34

This chapter stands in stark contrast to its predecessor. And it illustrates the consequences of revenge. While grace brings out the best in us, revenge brings out the worst in us—and we're never more unlike God than when we're plotting to get someone back.

This is what happened to Simeon and Levi. Because Shechem violated their sister, they lied and told him that if he and all the males in the city got circumcised, Shechem would be able to marry their sister. After they do so, Simeon and Levi come in and murder them. It's a punishment that far outweighs the crime—and a testimony to the results of revenge.

It's the opposite of what Esau did in the previous chapter. Instead of focusing on Jacob's wrongdoing, Esau trusted God with what was done to him and let it go. And God eventually replaced Esau's bitterness with grace.

That's not what happened to Simeon and Levi. And their enemies weren't the only ones who suffered. Ultimately Simeon and Levi did, too. They weren't honored by their father for their actions. They were criticized for being a disgrace.

And disgrace is the perfect word to end this chapter.

RESULTS OF REVENGE: GENESIS 34

Share

Warm-Up Qs

- Have you ever wanted to take revenge on someone? If so, how did you handle it?

- When someone has wronged you, what are some ways to handle it besides taking revenge?

- Have you ever regretted taking revenge on someone? What (if anything) did you do about it?

Observe

Observation Qs

- What was Leah's daughter's name? Where did she go in v. 1? What happened to her? (v. 2)

- What did Shechem feel for Dinah? (v. 3) What kind of relationship did he want with her? (v. 4)

- What did Shechem offer to do for Dinah? (vv. 11-12) How did Dinah's brothers respond? (vv. 13-15)

- What happened to Shechem and the rest of the men after they were circumcised? (v. 25) Who was responsible? How did Jacob respond? (v. 30)

Think

Interpretation Qs

- Do you suppose Shechem's sin with Dinah was an act of violence or love? (vv. 2-3) What does v. 19 tell you about Shechem's feelings for Dinah?

- Were Jacob's sons justified at all in regard to what they did? Or do you believe the punishment outweighed the crime?

- How does this chapter contrast with the previous chapter about Esau and Jacob?

- Why do you suppose Jacob was silent in this chapter until the end? Why did he let his sons take the lead in responding to the Shechemites? What does this tell you about Jacob?

Apply

Application Qs

- What lesson(s) do we learn about revenge in this chapter? What part of this story spoke to you the most?

- Have you ever been so angry with someone that you wanted to harm that person? If so, how did you handle it?

- Look at Romans 12:19-21. Do you abide by these verses in your life? If not, is there a relationship you have in which you can practice doing what these verses command?

- What do you think it means to "overcome evil with good"? Have you ever done this? Is there a situation or circumstance in your life in which you could do this right now?

Do

Optional Activity

For this activity, you'll need to make a cross from some small wooden beams and have some nails and paper. Distribute pieces of paper to the students in your group, and have them each write down the name of a person who's hurt them. Then have them write down one way they could pay back those people. If they are willing, have them fold their papers and nail them to the cross as a symbol of choosing to act in forgiveness and letting go of the desire for revenge.

QUIET TIME REFLECTIONS

Day 1: Genesis 34:1-4

- What word or phrase stands out to you from these verses? Why?

- Do you believe Shechem was in the wrong for what he did to Dinah? Where was he wrong in these verses? Where was he right?

- Spend time today thinking about God's desire for us to wait until after we are married to have sex.

Day 2: Genesis 34:5-7

- What word or phrase stands out to you from these verses? Why?

- Do you believe Dinah's brothers had a right to act the way they did in response to what happened to their sister—or were they overreacting?

- Spend time today thinking about how to let God temper our anger—even when it seems justified.

Day 3: Genesis 34:8-12

- What word or phrase stands out to you from this passage? Why?

- How did Hamor approach Jacob and his sons? Was he humble or tyrannical in his request?

- Spend time today thinking about how to forgive someone who's wronged you—especially if that person is trying to make things right.

Day 4: Genesis 34:13-17

- What word or phrase stands out to you from this passage? Why?

- How did Jacob's sons respond deceitfully in this passage?

Do you believe they planned on following through with their promise?

- Spend time today considering if you've ever made false promises. Why is it important to God that we keep our word?

Day 5: Genesis 34:18-24

- What word or phrase stands out to you from this passage? Why?

- How do you see Shechem's devotion to Dinah in this passage? How did they convince their people to be circumcised?

- Spend time today thinking about how revenge can have far-reaching negative effects.

Day 6: Genesis 34:25-31

- What word or phrase stands out to you from this passage? Why?

- How did Jacob respond to his sons for doing what they did? Do you believe Shechem really treated Dinah as a prostitute?

- Spend time today thinking about when you've acted in anger—and regretted it later.

Day 7: Genesis 34

Reread Genesis 34 and write out the verse or passage that stood out to you the most from this chapter. What did you learn from this story that you can apply to your life?

20. DIVINE DREAMS
Genesis 37

Joseph's dreams gave him a glimpse of his greatness—that one day everyone in his family would bow to him. If Joseph had been more thoughtful, he would have kept his dream to himself. Instead he shared it with exuberance.

Enraged, his brothers plotted to kill him and throw him in a cistern. By God's grace, they sold him as a slave instead.

This began a chain of events that led Joseph exactly to where he was meant to be. At every juncture in Joseph's story, God is at work in the bigger picture of his life.

The naive arrogance that characterized Joseph's early years would eventually be weeded out. He would be humbled many times. To be bound by your brothers, thrown into a cistern, and sold as a slave would make anyone rethink the way they handled their family relationships! Obviously his brothers' actions were wrong, but they were provoked by Joseph's egotism. And God knew that needed work.

So Joseph's journey would begin as a slave, continue as a prisoner, and end up as a prince.

Only God could pave a journey like that.

DIVINE DREAMS: GENESIS 37

Share

Warm-Up Qs

- What was the last dream you can remember? What made it memorable?

- Have you ever felt as though God spoke to you in a dream? If so, what do you think God's message to you was?

- When you compete with your siblings, do you usually come out ahead or behind? Does this affect your relationships with them?

Observe

Observation Qs

- What does v. 3 say about Joseph's relationship with his father? How does v. 4 describe his relationship with his brothers?

- What did Joseph do after having his dream? (v. 5) How did his brothers respond?

- What did Joseph's brothers plot to do in vv. 18-20? Which brother tried to rescue him in v. 21?

- What did the brothers do to Joseph's robe in vv. 31-32? What did Jacob think happened to Joseph? (v. 34) What really happened to Joseph? (v. 36)

Think

Interpretation Qs

- Do you believe Joseph should have told his brothers about his dream? Why/why not?

- Do you believe his brothers were justified in their anger toward Joseph? At what point in the story do you feel they overreacted?

- Why do you suppose Reuben had sympathy for Joseph? (vv. 21-22, 29-30)

- How do you see God's hand on Joseph's life in this chapter?

Apply

Application Qs

- Have you ever had a dream in which something good happens to you but something bad happens to someone else? If so, did you tell anyone about it?

- How would you respond if someone—perhaps a sibling—told you that he/she was destined for greatness?

- Is there anyone in your life whom you envy? Is it possible for you to be happy for that person instead? Why/why not?

- Have you ever experienced being favored over others? How can Joseph's journey help you deal with this if it happens in the future?

Do

Optional Activity

Go around your group and have each person share the last dream he/she remembers having. If any could interpret the dream as a message from God, what would that message be? Have other members help interpret the dreams. (Make it clear that you're only guessing; sometimes God speaks to us through our dreams, but our dreams also can be merely extensions and reflections of our thoughts, emotions, and fears.)

QUIET TIME REFLECTIONS

Day 1: Genesis 37:1-4

- What word or phrase stands out to you from these verses? Why?

- What do you notice about Jacob's relationship with Joseph in this passage? How do you think this affected the other brothers?

- Spend time today thinking about how favoritism affects relationships.

Day 2: Genesis 37:5-8

- What word or phrase stands out to you from these verses? Why?

- Do you believe Joseph should have shared his dream with his brothers? Why/why not?

- Spend time today thinking about what you should share with others, and what you should keep to yourself.

Day 3: Genesis 37:9-11

- What word or phrase stands out to you from these verses? Why?

- Do you believe Joseph was naive for sharing his other dream with his brothers?

- Spend time today thinking about how to learn from your mistakes—and not repeat them.

Day 4: Genesis 37:12-20

- What word or phrase stands out to you from this passage? Why?

- Do you believe Joseph's brothers had a right to be as angry as they were?

- Spend time today thinking about how anger can grow when we hold onto it and keep it inside.

Day 5: Genesis 37:21-28

- What word or phrase stands out to you from this passage? Why?

- Which two brothers showed Joseph grace? Why do you suppose they chose grace?

- Spend time today thinking about how you can love your sibling/s and not react with jealousy.

Day 6: Genesis 37:29-36

- What word or phrase stands out to you from this passage? Why?

- Which brother was in the dark about what happened to Joseph? How did Jacob respond?

- Spend time today thinking about how jealousy can tear apart families.

Day 7: Genesis 37

Reread Genesis 37 and write out the verse or passage that stood out to you the most from this chapter. What did you learn from this story that you can apply to your life?

21. TAMAR'S TENACITY
Genesis 38

Here we take a break from Joseph to follow Judah's story (who, incidentally, is within the genealogy of Christ). But the focus of the chapter is his daughter-in-law, Tamar.

Her two husbands killed for their wickedness, Tamar is a victim who is unjustly kept from having a child. She is promised a third husband, but the promise is never delivered. So Tamar decides to take her childbearing into her own hands.

After Judah's wife dies, Tamar covers her face and poses as a prostitute. We cringe at what happens next. A lonely widower, Judah wanders by, and not recognizing Tamar, he sleeps with her. Later when Judah finds out Tamar is pregnant, she is sentenced to death—until Judah finds out he's the father! Aware of his own sin, Judah realizes why Tamar did what she did. So she is forgiven and commended.

Tamar has her sons; and here's the surprise—they become part of the genealogy of Christ.

It's a story that proves we have a God who can turn a sinful plan into a sovereign plan. And only a big God can do that.

TAMAR'S TENACITY: GENESIS 38

Share

Warm-Up Qs

- Can you think of any situation in which it's okay to deceive in order to get something you want?

- Have you ever felt desperate enough to do something crazy? If so, what was it?

- When was the last time you tried to trick your parents? What happened?

Observe

Observation Qs

- How many children did Judah have? (vv. 2-5) Who did he get a wife for first? (v. 6) What was her name?

- Why did Er die? (v. 7) How did Judah help Tamar try to have children? (v. 8) Why didn't it work? (vv. 9-10)

- What did Judah promise Tamar in v. 11? Why did Tamar disguise herself in v. 14? What did Judah think about her? (vv. 15-16)

- What did Tamar keep as payment from Judah? (v. 18) What happened when Judah discovered Tamar was pregnant? (vv. 24-26)

Think

Interpretation Qs

- Why do you suppose Judah is hesitant to give his third son (Shelah) to Tamar? Do you understand his hesitation?

- Do you agree that what Tamar did to Judah was okay, given her circumstances? (vv. 13-18) Why/why not? Did Judah play any part in the wrongdoing?

- Do you believe Judah had a double standard when it came to punishment for prostitution? (v. 24) What does this tell you about the role of women in this culture?

- Why do you suppose Judah said Tamar was more righteous than him in v. 26? Do you believe she was?

Apply

Application Qs

- Do you believe what Tamar did in this chapter was wrong? Or was it okay in that culture in that time?

- Have you ever lied because someone (parent or teacher or other authority figure) treated you unfairly? If so, did you feel guilty about it?

- How do you feel about God including Tamar as one of five women listed in the genealogy of Christ? (Matthew 1:3) Do you believe this was strange for God to do?

- What does the story of Tamar teach you about God's grace? How can you apply it to your own life?

Do

Optional Activity

Split your small group in half and set up a debate. Half the group will argue why Tamar's actions were wrong; half the group will argue why Tamar's actions were justified. Let the debate go on for five minutes, and then as a group decide which side had the most compelling arguments. End by saying how God can redeem even our bad decisions when we decide to do what's right.

QUIET TIME REFLECTIONS

Day 1: Genesis 38:1-7

- What word or phrase stands out to you from this passage? Why?

- How did Tamar become Er's wife? Was it her choice?

- Spend time today thinking about whether you would prefer an arranged marriage or a marriage by choice.

Day 2: Genesis 38:8-12

- What word or phrase stands out to you from this passage? Why?

- How was Tamar a victim in this passage? Was anything that happened her fault?

- Spend time today thinking about how unfair things happen in life—but we always have a choice in regard to how we respond.

Day 3: Genesis 38:13-17

- What word or phrase stands out to you from this passage? Why?

- What motivated Tamar to do what she did in this passage? Do you believe she was wrong?

- Spend time today thinking about how the choices we make affect others.

Day 4: Genesis 38:18-23

- What word or phrase stands out to you from this passage? Why?

- How did Tamar show her intelligence in this passage? Does it seem as though Judah suspected anything at all?

- Spend time today thinking about how we can use our intelligence for good or for bad.

Day 5: Genesis 38:24-26

- What word or phrase stands out to you from these verses? Why?

- How did Judah take responsibility over what happened?

- Spend time today thinking about how important it is to own our part when we act wrongly.

Day 6: Genesis 38:28-30

- What word or phrase stands out to you from these verses? Why?

- How was the birth of Tamar's twins similar to the birth of Jacob and Esau? (Genesis 25)

- Spend time today thinking about how God takes our messy stories and works them together for good. (See Matthew 1:3.)

Day 7: Genesis 38

Reread Genesis 38 and write out the verse or passage that stood out to you the most from this chapter. What did you learn from this story that you can apply to your life?

22. JOSEPH AND POTIPHAR'S WIFE
Genesis 39

This chapter could be called "Desperate Housewife."

And under the pressure of that theme, Joseph has his first chance to shine.

Notice the subtle approach of Potiphar's wife. (v. 7) Joseph's response gives us our first lesson on avoiding temptation: Reaffirm the reasons why you shouldn't sin!

Listing your reasons for not giving in to temptation strengthens your resolve. That's what happened to Joseph, and he needed that strength for what was to come.

Verse 10 says Potiphar's wife spoke to him *day after day*. Can you imagine the strength that took? Finally she got so desperate, she grabbed his cloak and said, "Come to bed with me!"

Now Joseph is naked (or close to it) and a married woman stands in front of him. So he does what any respectable man would do.

He ran.

When temptation gets so great that you can't stand up to it, you always have the option to run. And sometimes that's what it takes. The apparent injustice of God is that Joseph ended up in jail after doing the right thing.

But focus on that word *apparent*—God's got Joseph's back.

JOSEPH AND POTIPHAR'S WIFE: GENESIS 39

Share

Warm-Up Qs

- What do you believe is the most difficult temptation to resist? Why?

- Have you ever been accused of something you didn't do? If so, what happened?

- What is the most unfair or unjust thing that's ever happened to you? How did you respond?

Observe

Observation Qs

- According to vv. 2-3, why did Joseph find favor with Potiphar? What did Potiphar do for Joseph because of this? (v. 4)

- What happened to Potiphar's household because of Joseph? (v. 5) How much did Potiphar concern himself with his household when Joseph was in charge?

- What did Potiphar's wife do to Joseph in v. 7? How did Joseph respond? (v. 9)

- How did Potiphar's wife trap Joseph in vv. 12-17? How did Potiphar respond? (vv. 19-20)

Think

Interpretation Qs

- What caused Joseph to prosper in Potiphar's household? Was it God's blessing or Joseph's behavior—or both?

- How did Joseph resist temptation from Potiphar's wife? What do we learn from his response to her?

- Why do you think Potiphar believed his wife instead of Joseph? Based on what you know of Joseph, do you believe he spoke out against the injustice—or just stayed silent?

- Look at what it says about Joseph's time in jail. (vv. 20-22) What's similar about his time in jail and the time he was with Potiphar?

Apply

Application Qs

- Do you believe you could be as strong as Joseph was in this chapter? What part of the story would have been hardest for you?

- What is the biggest temptation you've ever faced? How did you handle it?

- Is there any temptation you're dealing with now? If so, is there anything in this chapter that can help you deal with it?

- Have you ever experienced God giving you strength in the midst of temptation? If not, what could help you better rely on God's help? (Read 1 Corinthians 10:13.)

Do

Optional Activity

Have your students write down on pieces of paper their biggest temptations (anonymously). Then have them fold their papers and put it in a box. Have everyone draw one temptation from the box (if they draw their own, have them put it back and redraw). Then have them share strategies for resisting that temptation—what they would do to stay strong and resist. This is an indirect way for students to help each other win the battle of temptation. Close by reading James 1:15-17.

QUIET TIME REFLECTIONS

Day 1: Genesis 39:1-4

- What word or phrase stands out to you from these verses? Why?

- What do you observe about Joseph's relationship with Potiphar in these verses?

- Spend time today thinking about how you can be the best you can be in every relationship. Is there one you need to work on right now?

Day 2: Genesis 39:5-6

- What word or phrase stands out to you from these verses? Why?

- What do you observe about Joseph's relationship with God from these verses?

- Spend time today thinking about how God honors our behavior when we're doing our best.

Day 3: Genesis 39:7-10

- What word or phrase stands out to you from these verses? Why?

- What did Joseph do to stay strong while he was being tempted?

- Spend time today thinking about how reminding yourself of God's blessings helps you stay strong in the midst of temptation.

Day 4: Genesis 39:11-15

- What word or phrase stands out to you from this passage? Why?

- What do you learn about Potiphar's wife in these verses? What kind of woman was she?

- Spend time today thinking about your relationships with the opposite sex, and how important it is to choose wisely.

Day 5: Genesis 39:16-20

- What word or phrase stands out to you from this passage? Why?

- Why do you suppose Potiphar believed his wife even though she was lying? Do you believe Potiphar really knew her?

- Spend time today thinking about the importance of honesty in relationships.

Day 6: Genesis 39:21-23

- What word or phrase stands out to you from these verses? Why?

- How do you see the Lord caring for Joseph in these verses?

- Spend time today thinking about how God honors us when we do the right things—even if we're treated unjustly.

Day 7: Genesis 39

Reread Genesis 39 and write out the verse or passage that stood out to you the most from this chapter. What did you learn from this story that you can apply to your life?

23. TRUST THROUGH TRIALS
Genesis 40

Have you ever felt forgotten by God? This is the chapter for you. It represents the low point of Joseph's journey. As you read it, you'll see why.

Sometimes God works in ways that far surpass our understanding. That's what was happening to Joseph. From his perspective, he was abused and forgotten; but from God's perspective, Joseph was right where he needed to be.

Jail was the road that would lead Joseph to the palace. He just couldn't see it yet.

Never are we tempted to sin as much as when we feel God doesn't care. I'm sure that was how Joseph felt, at least from time to time. Yet his actions made the difference. By continuing to do the right thing, Joseph was setting himself up to be in the right place. And eventually his actions paid off.

We can imagine how hopeful Joseph was when the cupbearer left the jail and returned to the palace. (v. 14) But time passed, and Joseph's hope waned—it seemed certain he'd been forgotten.

But God hadn't forgotten Joseph. The cupbearer's memory would return.

And the timing would be perfect.

TRUST THROUGH TRIALS: GENESIS 40

Share

Warm-Up Qs

- Have you ever felt forgotten by God? If so, when?

- What's the hardest trial you've ever been through? What has been the hardest time of your life so far?

- Do you feel closer or farther from God when going through hard times? Why?

Observe

Observation Qs

- Who was with Joseph in prison? (vv. 1-2) Why were they in prison?

- What happened to the cupbearer and baker on the same night? (v. 5) What did Joseph observe about them? (vv. 7-8)

- Read vv. 9-19. Which of the two men had a good dream? Who had a bad dream?

- Did Joseph's interpretations come true? (vv. 21-22) What happened to the baker? What did the cupbearer remember about Joseph? (v. 23)

Think

Interpretation Qs

- What do you notice about Joseph's position in jail? (v. 4) How does this reveal God's presence in the midst of Joseph's trial?

- How was Joseph's ability to interpret dreams a gift from God? What did it do for him in jail?

- Before reading Joseph's interpretations, could you tell if the cupbearer's dream was a good one? (vv. 9-11) Why/why not?

Could you tell if the baker's dream was a bad one? (vv. 16-17) Why/why not?

- When do you believe Joseph figured out that the cupbearer forgot him? (v. 23) Do you believe Joseph felt forgotten by God? Why/why not?

Apply

Application Qs

- Do you find it difficult to trust God in the middle of a trial? Why/why not?

- Do you believe Joseph was confused at this point about the dreams he had in Genesis 37? What lessons do we learn from this chapter about God's plan and God's timing?

- Have you ever believed God was going to do something, and then something completely different happened? If so, how did you handle it?

- Is there a trial you're facing right now? If so, do you feel as though you can trust God with it? (See Isaiah 50:10.) Is there anything about what's happening that shows God is with you?

Do

Optional Activity

Pass out index cards and have everyone write down the most difficult trials they've experienced. Collect the cards. Debrief by talking about how we can't control what happens to us—but we can control how we respond. We have a choice between being a thermostat (setting the temperature of the room) or a thermometer (reacting to the temperature of the room). Then read through the index cards of trials and talk about what it would mean to respond as a thermometer, and then as a thermostat, in each trial.

QUIET TIME REFLECTIONS

Day 1: Genesis 40:1-4

- What word or phrase stands out to you from these verses? Why?

- How do you see God working in Joseph's circumstances in these verses?

- Spend time today thinking about how nothing happens by accident.

Day 2: Genesis 40:5-7

- What word or phrase stands out to you from these verses? Why?

- How did Joseph show his sensitivity to others in the midst of his own trial?

- Spend time today thinking about how you treat others when you're going through a hard time.

Day 3: Genesis 40:8-11

- What word or phrase stands out to you from these verses? Why?

- How did Joseph give credit to God for his gifts?

- Spend time today thinking about how you can give God the glory for your gifts and talents.

Day 4: Genesis 40:12-15

- What word or phrase stands out to you from these verses? Why?

- How did Joseph make the most of his opportunity in this passage?

- Spend time today thinking about how to make the most of every opportunity—but to leave the results to God.

Day 5: Genesis 40:16-19

- What word or phrase stands out to you from these verses? Why?

- In what ways was Joseph's honesty evident in these verses? Do you believe it was hard for him to tell the baker the interpretation of his dream?

- Spend time today thinking about how honest you are in your relationships. When are you most tempted to be dishonest?

Day 6: Genesis 40:20-23

- What word or phrase stands out to you from these verses? Why?

- When do you suppose Joseph realized the cupbearer had forgotten him? How do you suppose Joseph felt?

- Spend time today thinking about when you've felt forgotten or disappointed by someone. How did God provide you with strength and comfort?

Day 7: Genesis 40

Reread Genesis 40 and write out the verse or passage that stood out to you the most from this chapter. What did you learn from this story that you can apply to your life?

24. PERSEVERANCE PAYS OFF
Genesis 41

When two full years had passed . . .

Those are the first six words of this chapter. That means Joseph sat in jail for two full years. Can you imagine how he must have felt?

Joseph could have become bitter toward God and rejected his faith. Instead Joseph persevered and continued to trust when God wasn't doing what he wanted. And God honored him for that trust.

How many times Joseph must have questioned his journey. But here he finally was, seeing his dream come true. Joseph was a different man now; the prideful arrogance of his youth had been replaced by wisdom, humility, and strength. This was all part of God's plan. We finally see what his journey produced.

God allows us to go through times of suffering because our character is more important than our comfort. We might question why a good God would allow us to suffer; but God sees what the suffering can produce. We're on this earth not only to do God's will, but to become God's people. Suffering and endurance are what shape us most.

Just look at Joseph.

PERSEVERANCE PAYS OFF: GENESIS 41

Share

Warm-Up Qs

- Have you ever had something happen in your life that appeared bad at first but then turned out to be good?

- When you face difficulty, do you tend to be an optimist (thinking positively) or a pessimist (thinking negatively)?

- How good are you at waiting? On a scale of 1-10 (1 = very impatient, 10 = very patient), rate yourself when you have to wait for something.

Observe

Observation Qs

- How long was Joseph in jail when Pharaoh had his dream? (v. 1) What caused the cupbearer to remember Joseph? (vv. 8-9)

- Why did Pharaoh send for Joseph? (vv. 14-15) What did Joseph say about his ability to interpret dreams? (v. 16)

- What were the two dreams with the same meaning? (vv. 17-25) Why was the dream given in two forms? (v. 32)

- Why was Joseph put in charge of the palace? (vv. 39-40)

Think

Interpretation Qs

- After two years in jail, do you believe Joseph doubted he'd ever get out? Do you believe this time made Joseph better or worse as a person? Why?

- Do you believe the cupbearer felt badly about forgetting Joseph? (v. 9) How do you see God's providence in the cupbearer remembering Joseph at the time he did? Do you believe the timing was all part of God's plan?

- How was being in jail part of God's plan for getting Joseph in the palace? What does that tell you about the way God works?

- What similarities do you see between the way Joseph behaved in jail and his behavior in Pharaoh's palace? What does that tell you about Joseph?

Apply

Application Qs

- What does Joseph's journey from jail to the palace show you about the way God works in our lives? Do you believe God's more concerned with what happens in us or around us?

- If Joseph had gone straight to Pharaoh's palace after having his dream (in Genesis 37), how might things have been different for Joseph? Have you ever been glad about how a difficult circumstance changed you?

- What part of Joseph's story so far do you relate to most? Why?

- Would you say your life right now is more like Joseph in jail—or Joseph in the palace? Why?

Do

Optional Activity

Google *Nelson Mandela* and choose an article about his life that you can copy for your students. (The *Time* article from 1998 is good.) Read the article and have your students make a list of similarities between Nelson Mandela and Joseph (e.g., both went from prison to the palace and retained their character no matter where they were). As a bonus, rent *Invictus* and watch it with your group.

QUIET TIME REFLECTIONS

Day 1: Genesis 41:1-13

- What word or phrase stands out to you from this passage? Why?

- How is God's timing evident in these verses?

- Spend time today thinking about how God's timing is not the same as our timing—and God's timing usually means a longer wait for us!

Day 2: Genesis 41:14-24

- What word or phrase stands out to you from this passage? Why?

- How did Joseph give glory to God in front of Pharaoh? What does that tell you about Joseph's faith in spite of what he went through?

- Spend time today thinking about your relationship with God—is it the same in good times and bad times? If not, how is it different?

Day 3: Genesis 41:25-33

- What word or phrase stands out to you from this passage? Why?

- How did Joseph make the most of his opportunity in a humble way in this passage?

- Spend time today thinking about the difference between asserting yourself in a prideful way and asserting yourself with humility.

Day 4: Genesis 41:34-40

- What word or phrase stands out to you from this passage? Why?

- How was Joseph finally rewarded for all he'd been through? What was Pharaoh's reason for choosing him to rule under him?

- Spend time today thinking about the long-term rewards of following God through thick and thin.

Day 5: Genesis 41:41-49

- What word or phrase stands out to you from this passage? Why?

- How do you see Joseph's consistency of character in these verses? In what way did he act the same as when he was in prison or in the house of Potiphar?

- Spend time today thinking about the consistency of your character—do you behave the same way no matter what your surroundings or your circumstances?

Day 6: Genesis 41:50-57

- What word or phrase stands out to you from this passage? Why?

- How did Joseph's sons' names carry the story of Joseph's life?

- Spend time today thinking about how much you know and don't know about your parents' lives. If there is something you don't know, ask them!

Day 7: Genesis 41

Reread Genesis 41 and write out the verse or passage that stood out to you the most from this chapter. What did you learn from this story that you can apply to your life?

25. UNRECOGNIZED REUNION
Genesis 42

It's hard to imagine the emotions Joseph must have felt when he saw his brothers come to the door. The powerful leader Joseph had suddenly reverted to the little brother who was scorned years ago. That's not unusual when people come face-to-face with their pasts.

Seeing his brothers evoked many emotions in Joseph. We see those emotions in how he behaved. It all makes sense reading the story, but it must have been very confusing for Joseph's brothers. They wondered why they were being treated this way. Joseph was working out his childhood angst.

Perhaps the most touching scene was when the brothers decided they were being punished because of the way they mistreated Joseph. (v. 21) Joseph finally saw their remorse—and "he turned away from them and began to weep." (v. 24) Joseph's childhood wound was starting to heal.

When a wound begins to heal, initially it hurts. That's what happens when the treatment is applied. This is also true for emotional wounds.

And the Great Physician is treating Joseph's wound.

UNRECOGNIZED REUNION: GENESIS 42

Share

Warm-Up Qs

- Have you ever run into someone you haven't seen for a while and not recognized him/her?

- Have you ever made a change in your appearance and had others not recognize you?

- Have you ever carried a grudge against someone because of the way you were treated? If so, how did you handle it?

Observe

Observation Qs

- Why did Joseph's brothers go to Egypt? (vv. 1-3) Which of Joseph's brothers didn't go? (v. 4)

- What happened when Joseph's brothers saw him? (v. 6) Did they know who he was? (v. 8) What did Joseph call them? (v. 9)

- What did Joseph do to his brothers? (v. 17) What did he ask them to do to prove themselves? (vv. 19-20) Why did they reason this was happening to them? (v. 21)

- When the brothers went back to Jacob, what did they find in their sacks? (v. 34) How did Jacob respond to their request to take Benjamin? (v. 36)

Think

Interpretation Qs

- Why do you suppose Joseph's brothers didn't recognize him? (See Genesis 41:14, 42). How much time had passed since they last saw him?

- Why do you suppose Joseph lashed out at his brothers in v. 9? What emotions do you believe he might have been feeling?

- What do you suppose led Joseph to weep in v. 24?

- Why did Joseph want them to bring back Benjamin? (v. 15) What in this chapter shows you Joseph's unresolved conflict with his brothers?

Apply

Application Qs

- Have you ever been reunited with someone you haven't seen in a long time? If so, how did it feel?

- Is there anyone in your life who's difficult to be around? If so, what do you do when you see that person?

- When your brother or sister does something well, do you feel jealous or happy? Is there a relationship in your family that you need to work on?

- Have you ever had to face something from your past that was still painful in the present? If not, do you have a relationship that needs healing?

Do

Optional Activity

Have your students each bring a photo of themselves as children and give their photos to you. At the end of your meeting, put them all on a table and have everyone guess who is who. Who in your group looks the most like his or her photo? Who looks the least like his or her photo? Give the "Joseph Award" to the one who the group decides looks least like his or her photo.

QUIET TIME REFLECTIONS

Day 1: Genesis 42:1-5

- What word or phrase stands out to you from this passage? Why?

- How do you see God's timing and plan at work in this passage?

- Spend time today thinking about how God's plan is perfect—and often beyond what we can see in the moment with our human eyes.

Day 2: Genesis 42:6-10

- What word or phrase stands out to you from this passage? Why?

- What thought triggered Joseph's outburst of anger?

- Spend time today thinking about how our thoughts affect our emotions. If we dwell on our anger, we will be angry.

Day 3: Genesis 42:11-17

- What word or phrase stands out to you from this passage? Why?

- How was Joseph remembered by his brothers? What do they believe happened to him?

- Spend time today thinking about how well you know your family history. Do you know about your grandparents, uncles, and aunts? Is there anything you don't know about your family history?

Day 4: Genesis 42:18-24

- What word or phrase stands out to you from this passage? Why?

- What caused Joseph to weep in this passage?

- Spend time today thinking about any unresolved feelings you have about your family—is there anything that makes you sad? Angry? Resentful? If so, give those feelings to God.

Day 5: Genesis 42:25-35

- What word or phrase stands out to you from this passage? Why?

- Who did the brothers believe was responsible for the silver being in their sack? Why do you suppose they thought that?

- Spend time today thinking about anything hidden in your past that you feel guilty about. Are you willing to confess it and be free from your guilt? God is ready if you are.

Day 6: Genesis 42:36-38

- What word or phrase stands out to you from these verses? Why?

- How do you see Jacob's continued grief over Joseph? What was he afraid of in this passage?

- Spend time today thinking about your dad's love for you. Find a time to tell him you love him today.

Day 7: Genesis 42

Reread Genesis 42 and write out the verse or passage that stood out to you the most from this chapter. What did you learn from this story that you can apply to your life?

26. GRIEF AND PAYBACK
Genesis 43-44

The deeper the wound, the longer it takes to heal. When you scrape your knee, it only takes a few days for it to get better. When you break your leg, it takes a few months to heal.

It's hard to measure the depth of a wound in the heart. But these chapters show a heart wound takes some time to heal.

Joseph's brothers must have felt like pawns in a chess game. They kept being punished for crimes they didn't commit. But they were really being punished for what they did to Joseph. And this was Joseph's final act of revenge.

What happened next was a great confession from Joseph's brothers; and it came from their innocence and fear. It's a heart-wrenching plea—one that succeeded in finally melting Joseph's heart.

When Judah mentioned that Jacob still grieved for Joseph (44:28), I can only imagine how that made Joseph feel. The fact that Joseph was gone for so long and not forgotten must have touched his heart in unfamiliar ways. That's what finally breaks through to Joseph.

And the next chapter will show how he responds.

GRIEF AND PAYBACK: GENESIS 43-44

Share
Warm-Up Qs

- When you treat a wound and it hurts, is that a good sign or a bad sign? Why?

- How are emotional wounds similar to physical wounds? How are they different?

- Have you ever cried "happy" tears? If so, when?

Observe
Observation Qs

- Which of the brothers made himself personally responsible for Benjamin's safety? (43:8-9) What did Jacob tell the brothers to take with them? (vv. 11-13)

- Who did Joseph ask about when he saw his brothers again? (vv. 27-28) What did Joseph do when he saw Benjamin for the first time? (vv. 29-31) How did Joseph show his special affection for Benjamin in v. 34?

- What did Joseph tell the steward to do when his brothers left? (44:1-2) How did the brothers respond when they saw that Benjamin had the silver cup in his sack? (vv. 10-13)

- What does Joseph hear about himself in Judah's story? (vv. 27-28) What did Judah say will happen to Jacob if they don't bring Benjamin home? (vv. 30-31)

Think
Interpretation Qs

- Why do you suppose Jacob told his sons to take back to Joseph some of the best products in the land? (43:11) Does this remind you of how Jacob operated in the past?

- Why were Joseph's brothers astonished in v. 33? Were they flattered to be included at the table—or just wondering what was going on? How do you think they felt about Benjamin's portion? (v. 34)

- Why do you suppose Jacob's quoted in 44:27, saying his wife bore him two sons? Didn't Jacob have 12 sons and two wives? How do you suppose Joseph felt when Jacob said that?

- Why do you believe Joseph experienced such a long, slow reunion with his brothers? Do you believe he needed time to heal?

Apply

Application Qs

- Do you believe God wants to heal all our emotional wounds? Can you think of an emotional wound that God wants to heal in you?

- Have you ever tried to pay someone back for a wrong done to you? If so, how did it make you feel? Do you agree or disagree that we feel better when we take revenge?

- Has anyone ever done something to you that was (or is still) hard for you to forgive? If so, how did you handle it?

- Is there anyone you need to forgive right now? Is there anyone you need to ask forgiveness of?

Do

Optional Activity

Place Band-Aids of various sizes (tiny, small, medium, large, extra-large) on a table. Have your group members each focus on one emotional wound in their lives—things that happened in their homes, at school, with their friends, in class, in relationships with boyfriends/girlfriends. Tell them to choose the bandage size appropriate to cover the wound they're each carrying. Spend some time in prayer together, and let the students take their bandages home as symbols of God's desire to see their wounds healed.

QUIET TIME REFLECTIONS

Day 1: Genesis 43:1-14

- What word or phrase stands out to you from this passage? Why?

- Which brother took responsibility for safely bringing back Benjamin?

- Spend time today thinking about who in your family makes sacrifices for you. Do you need to love your family more sacrificially?

Day 2: Genesis 43:15-23

- What word or phrase stands out to you from this passage? Why?

- What was the difference between what was actually happening in this passage and the brothers' perspective on what was happening?

- Spend time today thinking about how we sometimes misjudge our circumstances because we don't have the full picture of what's going on.

Day 3: Genesis 43:24-34

- What word or phrase stands out to you from this passage? Why?

- Why did Joseph weep for a second time? What does this tell you about Joseph's heart for his family?

- Spend time today thinking about your relationships in your family. Which ones are good? Which ones need work?

Day 4: Genesis 44:1-10

- What word or phrase stands out to you from this passage? Why?

- What did Joseph's last trick tell you about what was going on inside him?

- Spend time today thinking about how hard it is to forgive someone when they've really hurt you.

Day 5: Genesis 44:11-26

- What word or phrase stands out to you from this passage? Why?

- How did Judah put himself on the line for his family? What does that tell you about his sense of responsibility?

- Spend time today thinking about whether or not you're willing to take risks to protect those you love.

Day 6: Genesis 44:27-34

- What word or phrase stands out to you from this passage? Why?

- How did Judah reveal how special Joseph was to his father in this passage?

- Spend time today thinking about how your parents show their love to you and your brothers and sisters.

Day 7: Genesis 43

Reread Genesis 43 and write out the verse or passage that stood out to you the most from this chapter. What did you learn from this story that you can apply to your life?

27. SEEING GOD'S PERSPECTIVE
Genesis 45

For three chapters Joseph punished his brothers for their past actions. Then the microscope was pulled away, and Joseph saw the wide-angle view. Viewing his circumstances from God's perspective, Joseph was finally ready to forgive.

The comfort Joseph imparted to his brothers made up for the grief he caused them. Joseph not only extended forgiveness; he reinterpreted their actions as good—in light of the bigger picture. (v. 5) This shows how mature Joseph's faith had become.

Through pain and perseverance, Joseph was tested and tried—and he emerged victorious. The words he spoke to his brothers in this chapter are a far cry from the words he spoke to them years ago. Then he was a proud, haughty little brother; here he was a mature man of God.

Overhearing Joseph's speech, the palace officials reported the news to Pharaoh, who responded by offering Joseph's brothers his best land. Here we see the rippling effect of grace: When grace spills over from our hearts, it touches everyone around us.

And this story has enough grace to touch us all.

SEEING GOD'S PERSPECTIVE: GENESIS 45

Share

Warm-Up Qs

- Why do you suppose God allows bad things to happen in our lives?

- Do you believe we see things from the past differently when we look back on our lives? If so, what changed?

- Do you feel as though your perspective and God's perspective are the same? If not, how are they different?

Observe

Observation Qs

- When Joseph revealed himself to his brothers, how did they respond? (v. 3)

- Why did Joseph say he was sent to Egypt? (vv. 5-7) Who did he say was ultimately responsible for what happened to him? (v. 8)

- How did Pharaoh react to the news that Joseph's brothers had come? (v. 16) What did he tell Joseph he would provide for his family if they came to Egypt? (v. 18) What were they given for their journey? (v. 19)

- How did Jacob respond when his sons told him about Joseph? (v. 26) What convinced him they were telling the truth? (vv. 27-28)

Think

Interpretation Qs

- Why do you suppose Joseph's brothers were terrified when Joseph revealed who he was? (v. 3) What thoughts must have been going through their heads?

- How did Joseph reinterpret his past in this chapter? (vv. 5-8) What does this reveal to you about Joseph's relationship with God?

- How had Joseph changed since he last talked to his brothers about his dreams in Genesis 37? What do you think caused this change?

- How do you see God's provision for the Israelites in this story of Joseph? What does it tell you about the way God works?

Apply

Application Qs

- Has something bad ever happened to you that God used for good? If so, what?

- Have you ever experienced something that God used to help others?

- What does this chapter teach you about the way God works in our lives? Is there anything about Joseph's story you can apply to your own life?

- Is there an area of your life right now for which you need God's perspective? How can this story encourage you?

Do

Optional Activity

Find a microscope and either bring it to your meeting or take your group to the microscope. Put a few objects underneath the microscope and invite each of your students to look at them through the lens—and then without the magnification. Tell them to describe the difference in how the object looks. Make the connection that often we're looking at our lives through a microscope, but God also sees the bigger view. When we pull back, we get a glimpse of God's perspective—and we understand more of what God has been doing in our lives (and in the lives of those around us).

QUIET TIME REFLECTIONS

Day 1: Genesis 45:1-3

- What word or phrase stands out to you from these verses? Why?

- What was the brothers' first response to Joseph's revelation?

- Spend time today thinking about when you were shocked to see someone. How did you react?

Day 2: Genesis 45:4-8

- What word or phrase stands out to you from this passage? Why?

- How did Joseph give his brothers another perspective on what they did to him years ago? How do you suppose they felt?

- Spend time today thinking about someone who made you feel better about something bad you did.

Day 3: Genesis 45:9-13

- What word or phrase stands out to you from this passage? Why?

- What did Joseph offer his brothers? What does that tell you about the condition of Joseph's heart?

- Spend time today thinking about what real forgiveness means. Is there anyone you need to forgive?

Day 4: Genesis 45:14-15

- What word or phrase stands out to you from these verses? Why?

- How do you see grace exemplified in these verses? What did Joseph do with his brothers before they talked?

- Spend time today thinking about the importance of hugs and affection as part of the act of forgiveness.

Day 5: Genesis 45:16-20

- What word or phrase stands out to you from this passage? Why?

- How did Joseph's grace spill over to Pharaoh? What did he offer Joseph's brothers?

- Spend time today thinking about the far-reaching effects of grace.

Day 6: Genesis 45:21-28

- What word or phrase stands out to you from this passage? Why?

- How did Jacob respond when he found out Joseph was alive?

- Spend time today thinking about when you learned about something that changed your perspective and gave you hope.

Day 7: Genesis 45

Reread Genesis 45 and write out the verse or passage that stood out to you the most from this chapter. What did you learn from this story that you can apply to your life?

28. AUTHORITY FROM GOD
Genesis 47

The man who held the highest authority in Egypt was Pharaoh. Some people regarded him as a god. Even Joseph, with all his might and majesty, was subject to him. And that's what makes the events of this chapter so intriguing.

Pharaoh gave Joseph's family permission to settle in one of the best territories in Egypt. But it's what happens next that stands out as a surprise: Joseph presented his father to Pharaoh, and v. 7 says "Jacob blessed Pharaoh." Here was the most powerful figure in all of Egypt being "blessed" by an old Jewish patriarch. I'm sure there was a moment where Joseph flinched, perhaps embarrassed by his dad's actions. But Pharaoh didn't reject it, which might be the biggest surprise of all.

The picture of this old Jewish man blessing this powerful king is one worth pondering: At that moment, Jacob established his authority as different from Pharaoh's. And Pharaoh accepted the blessing with grace.

It's a small glimpse into the difference between earthly power and heavenly power. And it sets the tone for the coming king.

Instead of sitting on a throne, this king would hang from a cross. And from there, he would reign over all.

AUTHORITY FROM GOD: GENESIS 47

Share

Warm-Up Qs

- Who in your life has authority over you? What gives them that authority?

- When you think of powerful people, what individuals come to mind?

- How would you compare earthly power with heavenly power? Are they the same? If not, how are they different?

Observe

Observation Qs

- What occupation did Joseph's brothers hold? (v. 3) Where did they tell Pharaoh they wanted to settle? (v. 4)

- When Joseph brought Jacob before Pharaoh, what did Jacob do? (v. 7) What question did Pharaoh ask Jacob? (v. 8) How did Jacob respond? (v. 9)

- What happened to people's money because of the famine in Egypt? (vv. 14-15) What did Joseph take as alternate payment? (vv. 16-17)

- How did Joseph end up buying all the land in Egypt? (vv. 18-20) What did Joseph promise his father at the end of his life? (vv. 29-31)

Think

Interpretation Qs

- How do you imagine Pharaoh felt when Jacob blessed him? (v. 7) How do you imagine Joseph felt?

- What was the difference between Pharaoh's authority and Jacob's authority? Whose was greater? Why?

- How did Joseph show his continued loyalty to Pharaoh in this chapter? (vv. 20-26) How was his behavior similar to the way he conducted himself at Potiphar's house and in jail?

- Why do you suppose it was important to Jacob that he was not buried in Egypt?

Apply

Application Qs

- Have you ever observed someone who seemed to have authority from God? If so, what did that authority look like?

- Who is the most powerful person you have ever met? What made that person powerful?

- If you were given the choice, would you choose earthly power or heavenly power? Why?

- In this chapter, Joseph displayed humility and strength in his power. Which of these qualities do you need most in your life right now?

Do

Optional Activity

Have your students make a list of all the people with authority over them (parents, teachers, coaches, youth pastor, pastor, police, mayor, governor, president). Then have them rank their authority and determine which individuals have the most to the least authority in their lives. Finally have them circle the people who have their authority from God, and the people who have their authority from humans. Which is the greater authority?

QUIET TIME REFLECTIONS

Day 1: Genesis 47:1-6

- What word or phrase stands out to you from this passage? Why?

- How did Pharaoh pass his authority over to Joseph in this passage?

- Spend time today thinking about how carrying out your responsibilities will give you more authority in your life.

Day 2: Genesis 47:7-12

- What word or phrase stands out to you from this passage? Why?

- What did Jacob do when he saw Pharaoh? How do you suppose Joseph felt?

- Spend time today thinking about the authority figures in your life, and who has the most authority.

Day 3: Genesis 47:13-17

- What word or phrase stands out to you from this passage? Why?

- How did Joseph show his wisdom as a businessman in this passage?

- Spend time today thinking about how to do your best in all of your jobs, no matter how small. Your performance now will impact the way you perform when the job is bigger.

Day 4: Genesis 47:18-22

- What word or phrase stands out to you from this passage? Why?

- How did Joseph show his respect for God in the way he treated the priests' land?

- Spend time today thinking about how you show your respect for God through your actions.

Day 5: Genesis 47:23-26

- What word or phrase stands out to you from these verses? Why?

- How did Joseph show his loyalty to Pharaoh in these verses?

- Spend time today thinking about how you can show your loyalty to people in authority over you.

Day 6: Genesis 47:27-31

- What word or phrase stands out to you from this passage? Why?

- What was Jacob's dying request? Why do you believe this was important to him?

- Spend time today thinking about what might prove important when you get to the end of your life.

Day 7: Genesis 47

Reread Genesis 47 and write out the verse or passage that stood out to you the most from this chapter. What did you learn from this story that you can apply to your life?

29. A SHADOW OF THINGS TO COME
Genesis 49

In this chapter, we get our first glimpse of Jesus. And it comes from a dying man's words. It's a bit puzzling why Jacob's fourth son would carry the honor of producing the coming king. But as the chapter unfolds, we see why.

Reuben, the eldest son, seems the logical choice—but Reuben has defiled his father's bed. Simeon and Levi are next in line to receive Jacob's blessing, but the circumstances covered in Genesis 34 have darkened their pasts. And so, Judah is chosen.

Jacob goes on to bless his other sons; and his words not only are for them, but also for their descendants. Jacob's sons will become the 12 tribes of Israel, and the words of this chapter reveal how these tribes began.

As we've seen before in Genesis, God's plan works in concert with our choices. Jacob's prophecy shows a combination of both. There were consequences and rewards for each son according to their behavior. (v. 28) But grace was present also.

It's found in the fourth son's blessing. He received the kingdom merely because he was next in line.

It's the first glimpse that God's kingdom would not be earned, but simply given.

And Judah would experience this grace first.

A SHADOW OF THINGS TO COME: GENESIS 49

Share

Warm-Up Qs

- Have your parents ever shared a dream they had for your life? If so, what was it?

- If you had to describe each of your brothers and sisters with one word, what would those words be?

- If someone asked you today what you wanted to be when you grew up, how would you respond?

Observe

Observation Qs

- Why did Jacob gather his sons? (v. 1) What two names did he call himself in v. 2?

- Why did Jacob say Reuben would no longer excel? (v. 4) Why did Jacob curse Simeon and Levi? (v. 7)

- What did Jacob call Judah in v. 9? What prophecy did he give concerning Judah? (v. 10)

- According to Jacob, whose hand of blessing was on Joseph? (vv. 24-25) How did Joseph show his strength? (vv. 23-24) What blessing did Jacob give Joseph? (v. 26)

Think

Interpretation Qs

- Why do you believe Judah was chosen to carry the seed of the future king? (v. 10) (Also see Matthew 1:3). Was it because he was greater than his brothers?

- Do you believe Jacob's blessings to his sons were fair? Did Reuben, Simeon, and Levi deserve what was said about them?

- How did Jacob's blessings show that God rewards faithfulness?

- Why did Jacob tell Judah that his father's sons will bow to him? (v. 8) How is his power different from Joseph's? (v. 26)

Apply

Application Qs

- How is the way Judah received God's kingdom similar to the way we receive God's kingdom? Do we do anything to earn it? Why/why not?

- Have you ever received a blessing from your parents? (e.g., it could be an affirmation, a word of confidence or support, etc.) If so, what was it? If not, what do you wish they would say?

- If you could choose just one of Jacob's blessings to be applied to your life, which one would you choose?

- How much of what happens to us is up to God, and how much is up to us? Do you believe our behavior impacts God's will? If so, how?

Do

Optional Activity

Give your students a chance to write their own epitaphs—a short paragraph about their lives and the way they want to be remembered. In this chapter, Jacob blessed his sons with a word about what will happen to them—and this is an opportunity for students to do that for themselves. Give your students five minutes and then let them read their epitaphs to the group.

QUIET TIME REFLECTIONS

Day 1: Genesis 49:1-4

- What word or phrase stands out to you from these verses? Why?

- Why did Jacob say Reuben would no longer excel as the oldest son?

- Spend time today thinking about how our choices can produce long-term effects.

Day 2: Genesis 49:5-7

- What word or phrase stands out to you from these verses? Why?

- How is this passage a reference to Genesis 34?

- Spend time today thinking about how revenge can ruin our lives.

Day 3: Genesis 49:8-12

- What word or phrase stands out to you from this passage? Why?

- How is Christ alluded to in these verses? What part does Judah have in Christ's coming? (Look at Matthew 1:3)

- Spend time today thinking about how Christ's coming was predicted throughout the Old Testament.

Day 4: Genesis 49:13-21

- What word or phrase stands out to you from this passage? Why?

- What do you believe is the most positive prophecy in these verses? Which is the most negative?

- Spend time today thinking about what you'd like to be said about your life.

Day 5: Genesis 49:22-26

- What word or phrase stands out to you from this passage? Why?

- What did Jacob say about Joseph's relationship with God in these verses? How was Joseph's life a testimony to God's presence in him?

- Spend time today thinking about your relationship with God and how it affects who you are and what you do.

Day 6: Genesis 49:27-33

- What word or phrase stands out to you from this passage? Why?

- What does v. 28 say about Jacob's blessings for his sons?

- Spend time today thinking about what your father would say about you right now. Would he say words of promise or words of warning?

Day 7: Genesis 49

Reread Genesis 49 and write out the verse or passage that stood out to you the most from this chapter. What did you learn from this story that you can apply to your life?

30. GOD'S PURPOSE REVEALED
Genesis 50

There is only one way to see all that God has done in our lives. It happens as we look back. By looking in the rearview mirror of our lives, we see clearly what's behind us. And in this chapter Joseph does just that.

Joseph went from being scorned by his brothers to living as a slave and then to sitting forgotten as a prisoner. Yet it was that very road that led him to Pharaoh's palace. Just at the right time, Joseph was able to use his gifts to provide for the futures of thousands of people. But that road contained a lot of pain.

Yet God never wastes pain that's allowed into our lives. And while we don't always know the reasons for the pain, we know God has a purpose in it. The question is: *Does God really understand how it feels?*

Those of us who've lived after Jesus know the answer to that question. It comes when we look to the cross. No matter how much we suffer, we'll never suffer more than Jesus.

And Joseph's story shows us that God is big enough to see us through.

GOD'S PURPOSE REVEALED: GENESIS 50

Share

Warm-Up Qs

- When was the last time you did something that got you into trouble? What happened?

- Have you ever expected to be punished for something and were forgiven instead?

- Do you believe it's fair to be punished for something that happened in the distant past? Why/why not?

Observe

Observation Qs

- What did Joseph direct his physicians to do with his father? (v. 2) How long did the Egyptians mourn for Jacob? (v. 3)

- Who accompanied Joseph when he left to bury his father? (vv. 7-8) Who remained in Goshen?

- What were Joseph's brothers worried about in v. 15? What message did they send him? What did Joseph do when he received the message?

- What did Joseph say was the difference between his brothers' intentions and God's intentions? (v. 20) How did he reassure them? What oath did he make his brothers swear before he died?

Think

Interpretation Qs

- What evidence of Joseph's love for his father do you observe in this chapter? In what ways do you detect Pharaoh's support of Joseph?

- What evidence do you see of the Egyptians' love and respect for Joseph when his father died? What does that tell you about Joseph?

- Why do you believe Joseph wept when he got the message from his brothers? (v. 17) What does Joseph's response tell you about his relationship with God? (vv. 19-21)

- How does Joseph foreshadow future events in v. 24? How does he pass on his faith?

Apply

Application Qs

- Have you ever looked back on something that happened and saw God's purpose in it? If so, how did it change your perspective?

- Would you be willing to make a sacrifice in your own life for the greater good of others? Why/why not?

- What is the greatest lesson you've learned from Joseph's life? What specifically have you gleaned for application to your own life (and circumstances)?

- In what area of your life do you need to trust God more? How does the story of Joseph help you to do that?

Do

Optional Activity

Find some bicycle rearview mirrors for everyone in your group. (You can get them at Target or Kmart.) Pass them out to your students as a symbol for how they can view God's work in their lives (i.e., we only see what God is up to when we look back! Only then is God's purpose revealed).

QUIET TIME REFLECTIONS

Day 1: Genesis 50:1-6

- What word or phrase stands out to you from this passage? Why?

- How did Joseph keep his word to his father?

- Spend time today thinking about the importance of keeping a promise.

Day 2: Genesis 50:7-9

- What word or phrase stands out to you from these verses? Why?

- What facts best support how important and respected Joseph was to the Egyptians in these verses?

- Spend time today thinking about your reputation among the people around you. If something happened to you, would there be people there to support you?

Day 3: Genesis 50:10-14

- What word or phrase stands out to you from this passage? Why?

- Who mourned for Jacob? How long did they mourn?

- Spend time today thinking about the time we need to spend mourning when we experience loss. Is there any loss you need to mourn right now?

Day 4: Genesis 50:15-17

- What word or phrase stands out to you from these verses? Why?

- What were the brothers afraid of after their father died?

- Spend time today pondering if you've ever been afraid of what someone might do to you.

Day 5: Genesis 50:18-21

- What word or phrase stands out to you from these verses? Why?

- How did Joseph show his trust and faith in God through his response to his brothers?

- Spend time today thinking about whether you trust God to work out all things for good.

Day 6: Genesis 50:22-26

- What word or phrase stands out to you from this passage? Why?

- What promise did Joseph make to the Israelites on his deathbed? Under whose leadership did this promise come true? (see Exodus 3)

- Spend time today thinking about how God's perspective is so much bigger than ours—and that our lives are just a part of God's story!

Day 7: Genesis 50

Reread Genesis 50 and write out the verse or passage that stood out to you the most from this chapter. What did you learn from this story that you can apply to your life?